Fire on the River

The Defense of the
World's Longest Covered Bridge
and How It Changed
the Battle of Gettysburg

George Sheldon

QHP

QUAKER HILLS PRESS INCORPORATED
LANCASTER, PA

Copyright ©2006 by George Sheldon.

PUBLISHED BY
QUAKER HILLS PRESS INCORPORATED.
Post Office Box 6238
Lancaster, PA 17607-6238

Phone: 888-225-7110

http://www.quakerhills.com

ISBN # 0-9779315-0-1, 978-0-9779315-0-7

Library of Congress Control Number: 2006903023

About the Cover Art

Jason Getz, a Lancaster County native and graphics arts student, created the depiction of the fire on the Susquehanna River on June 28, 1863. A student at Lampeter-Strasburg High School and member of the Class of 2007, this is the first publication of Jason's art.

Contents

Acknowledgements

No book is ever completed without the help of others. During the process of creating a volume, there are many people that assist an author. This book is no exception.

I want to thank everyone that assisted me in making this book a reality. From the residents of Columbia and Wrightsville, who stopped and talked to me for a few minutes during my different visits to the area while researching this book, to those that provided specific information that I needed. Sometimes, the smallest piece of data is what is needed to fit together the puzzle.

Special thanks to the staffs of the Lancaster County Library, the Columbia Public Library Association, and Pennsylvania State Library, the Pennsylvania Archives, and the Military History Museum in Carlisle. The library staff at the Millersville University also assisted me with several questions. Sometimes the help is just to retrieve a box of microfilm, while other times it is more specific, suggesting places to look for specific information. Whatever my requests, the various librarians and staffs were always cheerfully helpful. I really do appreciate their work and assistance. We should all support librarians, and never forget their quiet work.

I especially appreciate the help I received from the Columbia Historic Preservation Society and the Lancaster County Historic Society. They were great sources of information and assistance.

The information made available by the Pennsylvania Historical and Museum Commission served as a base for the launch of many sections of this book. I appreciated using the Commission's information as a springboard into other regions.

United States Representative Joseph R. Pitts assisted me by providing copies of important research documents. I appreciate his kind assistance and help.

Special thanks to Ronald C. Young, author of *Lancaster County Pennsylvania in the Civil War*. His suggestions and advice helped make this a better book.

Thanks to Jason Getz for his work on the art used on the cover.

I want to send a very special thank you to Scott Mingus. His expertise and keen eye helped to make this a far better book. I appreciate his efforts in assisting me during the final edits.

Mickey Kraft of the Lancaster Civil War Roundtable also contributed to the final book here in your hands. Her suggestions and help cannot go unrecognized. I appreciate all your assistance.

Preface

Great scholars of the U.S. Civil War disagree on the importance of the burning the Columbia-Wrightsville Bridge in late June, 1863. Some of these most learned individuals say it stopped the advance of the Confederates, preventing them from capturing Lancaster, Harrisburg, and Philadelphia. Others argue effectively that it was a mere sideshow before the great Battle of Gettysburg.

No one can doubt the significance of the transportation system launched at this crucial place in southeastern Pennsylvania, especially in 1863. By this time, Columbia had established an intersection of roads, canals, and railroads to York, Lancaster, and the state capital of Harrisburg. These links provided connections to the bigger cities that were beyond, such as Philadelphia to the east, New York to the northeast, and Baltimore-Washington to the southwest.

Barge traffic by a network of local canals had faded, but still existed. Railroads had not yet killed the canal system. The mighty Pennsylvania Railroad recognized Columbia as a key intersection in moving freight and passengers to various points.

In June 1863, a grand bridge spanned the Susquehanna River. At the time, it was the longest covered bridge in the world. It connected the eastern shore of the Susquehanna, at Columbia, Lancaster County, to the western shore, at Wrightsville, York County.

The military generals, skilled at reading maps, also knew the vital importance of this key link, strategically located along one of the widest portions of the sometimes roaring Susquehanna River. To the Southerners, it was a strategic point, one to capture and control. To the Northerners, it was a tactical gateway that needed defended and protected, at all costs.

As the Confederate forces moved toward the great bridge that crossed the Susquehanna, a hurriedly assembled, ill-equipped, and inadequately trained group of state militia and local citizens turned volunteers was the only thing protecting it from the battle-hardened Southerners.

This is the story of that well-built bridge – and how the local civilians defended it. Many wore fresh, blue Union uniforms, but they were, for the most part, still civilians. With little military training, they were citizen volunteers, a ragtag force of local militia, consisting of farmers, laborers, and students. In most history books, there is little more than a paragraph devoted to the Wrightsville skirmish. It is mostly forgotten, because of the great Battle of Gettysburg that occurred three days later. There is not much mentioned about the Columbia-Wrightsville Bridge, its defenders, and the eventual loss of the bridge.

It is a story of how the invading Confederates first wanted to burn the bridge, and then decided to capture it. It is a story of how the Federals wanted to defend the bridge, and only prevent the Southerners from crossing it, keeping it mostly intact, but ended destroying it.

It is a story of how some of the first colored men served in the Civil War, and how they did excellent service to defend the United States. Technically, they were not soldiers as they were not sworn into duty and wore no uniforms. At best, they were an informal local militia. They had no military training or experience. They were civilians with an odd assortment of guns, and admirable courage.

It is a story of how a private company owned a bridge that was destroyed by the U.S. Military. Congress never paid a dollar for the loss.

It is also a story full of what if's? What if the Confederates had gained control of this bridge? What if General Early had advanced to Lancaster? Would the Battle of Gettysburg had occurred? Would Harrisburg been taken?

It is a story about the day there was a great fire on the river. This book is an attempt to offer some insight into what happened there, just days before the Battle of Gettysburg. Here is the story of some Americans and what happened in June 1863, and what has been mostly forgotten.

George Sheldon
Lancaster, PA

Chapter 1
The Confederate Invasion

The dusty limestone powder of the county's roads lodged in the throats of the marching Southerners. The best defense against the coarse grit's irritation was a good chew of tobacco. The battle-hardened Confederates, looking ragged and worn, were too far away from a good source of those fine Southern tobacco plugs. They marched forward, following simple orders and the men in front of them. Thirsty and parched, the ragtag force pounded their battered and tired feet into the hardened dirt road, creating a hypnotizing rhythm. Their self-induced trance made the march easier, their dry throats less irritating, and their sore feet less painful.

Without noticing their exact position, this portion of the Confederate army crossed over the mostly unmarked Mason-Dixon Line, leaving neutral soil. As they traversed the shared boundary of Maryland and Pennsylvania, the thirsty Southerners became an invading force. No longer defending the soil of the states that had seceded from the Union, the Army of Northern Virginia plodded north. Soldiers from various southern states made up the massive force. Some of the infantry marched onward with tattered, worn shoes and boots, while others were barefoot and had no leather to protect their calloused feet. The northern invasion by the Army of Northern Virginia was well underway.

That Pennsylvania summer day had warmth. The valleys of the Pennsylvania countryside overflowed with plush greens as the summer plants pushed their plentiful foliage. The marching men saw cornfields filled with knee-high, bright light green plants. Golden amber colors were present in the abundant wheat fields. It was gentle, pleasant land. Sweet smells of honeysuckle and corn permeated the warming summer air. Red large barns carefully situated on the large plots of tilled soil reminded some of the men of their native Virginia, the way it was before the War started. Since then, their once gentle state had turned into a crossroads used by the armies of the North and South. Productive farmland had been transformed into deadly battlefields. The northern valleys of Virginia were once so much like this beautiful Pennsylvania land. American politics and lines drawn decades before on flimsy maps is what made the difference in these two similar geographic regions. The valleys of both states had once been so similar, so productive, and so satisfying.

It was a beautiful, early summer Tuesday in southeastern Pennsylvania.

Thousands of men wearing gray and butternut suits marched forward, unchallenged in any respect. Their columns, intimidating by the sheer size and numbers, the men of the Army of Northern Virginia pushed north and east. These Southern soldiers, looking motley and unkempt, were tough and unbreakable.

It was June 23, 1863.

A forty-six year old lawyer from Virginia commanded this portion of the invading Southern force. Jubal Early, a man with a biblical name, was anything but like the Bible. A staunch and resolute Confederate, tough as saddle leather, with a ferocious bark, and a reputation for a fierce bite, he was known as Old Jube.

The Confederate General, always sarcastic, abrasive, and righteous, perched high on his mount, but rode slightly bent. He was always particular about the cut and fit of his clothes. His gray articulate uniform, formfitting and perfectly tailored, ornate with gold braid, made his weathered face even scarier.

The General drew quick attention his harsh, intimidating facial features. With piercing eyes, Jube intensely and immediately stared anyone down. These days, he seldom bothered to trim his full beard. It was graying and scruffy. The pain from his chronic rheumatism twisted him, and made him stoop as he walked, and as he rode his horse.

Fellow Confederate General Stonewall Jackson had also trusted Jubal Early. He was the only man known to swear in front of General Robert E. Lee. Everyone else refrained from such language when in the presence of the commanding Southern general. Not General Early. He was no Southern gentleman. Often General Lee referred to Jubal Early as "my bad old man."

General Lee had ordered General Early to take his men northward. It was part of the Confederate commander's overall plan to force the Federal army to leave Washington, DC, in pursuit of the Southerners. Lee set into motion the movement of 75,000 gray coats north, into Pennsylvania. It was a well-planned, major invasion.

General Early's force was just one part of the invading Southern army. The target was southern Pennsylvania. First, the Confederates planned to move into the rich farmland of Cumberland Valley, then east through York, cutting railroad and transportation lines. From there, General Early would turn his force toward Harrisburg, the state's capital city. Then the Southerners would move east, on to Philadelphia, forcing a Federal surrender, and a Confederate victory. With Harrisburg and Philadelphia controlled by the Confederates, President Lincoln would have to discuss peace terms with the South, and recognize the Confederate States of America as its own sovereign nation.

Born in the Red Valley section of Franklin County, Virginia on November 3, 1816, Jubal Early had graduated from the United States Military Academy at West Point in 1837. It was at West Point where he first met another future Confederate General, Lewis Armistead. One afternoon, after taunting Armistead, Jubal Early was on the receiving end of a whack over the head with a mess hall plate. As a result of the assault, Armistead was expelled from the academy. The youngest of three sons, Jubal Early knew how to bait someone to get what he wanted. He would make a sacrifice, including his own head, to have what he truly wanted. Trust old Jube just like you trust a coiled, cornered rattlesnake, with its tail shaking.

The young Early did well enough at West Point with his studies to be selected into the artillery. At the time, the Army's artillery had second pick of the graduates. He was eighteenth in his class out of 50.

After a year of service in the artillery, Jubal Early left the army and took up the study of law. He was soon involved in politics. It was not long before he was serving in the Virginia legislature. From 1842 to 1852, he served as the Commonwealth Attorney of Virginia. His service as the State's Attorney was interrupted in 1847 and 1848 when he participated in the Mexican War as a major of the Virginia volunteers. He returned to Virginia following the war and returned to his law practice. He remained involved in politics.

As the War Between the States became more likely, a convention was called to determine the true position of the State in the impending conflict. Jubal Early voted against secession at the Virginia Secession Convention. As the Federal government started to make aggressive moves, Jubal Early's passion for his state was aroused. Early, who had been opposed at first to the succession, found that his loyalty to the state was greater than his loyalty to the Union.

Jubal Early decided that he would pull his sword to defend his beloved Virginia. He immediately joined the Confederate army when Virginia seceded from the Union.

When the Civil War began, Jubal Early became the Colonel of the 24th Virginia Infantry Regiment. Early led a brigade at First Manassas[1]. His service at Bull Run impressed his superiors so much that he was appointed a brigadier general. Early's brigade moved then to defend against Union General George B. McClellan's Peninsula Campaign. McClellan had devised a master plan where he would take the Army of the Potomac, sail it south to the Peninsula between the James and York Rivers, and rapidly march onto Richmond. There, he would capture the southern capital, and end the rebellion.

While leading a charge against Federal forces at Williamsburg, Brigadier General Early was shot in the shoulder. He was able to recover from his wound and return to action at Malvern Hill. Although still recuperating from his injury, he returned to duty after he heard that a battle was imminent in front of Richmond. He arrived in time to command a new brigade. He was still weak and nearly disabled from his shoulder wound. He needed assistance to mount his horse.

Early then fought at Second Manassas. He led Confederate Major General Richard Ewell's division at Antietam. He defended the heights during the Battle of Fredericksburg. Jubal Early proved he was tough, even under fierce Federal bombardment.

After the Battle of Fredericksburg, the one star General Early received a long overdue promotion to major general. Although the division was still being called, "Ewell's Division," it was per-

---

[1] Also known as the Battle of Bull Run

manently turned over to General Early with General Ewell's blessing. The non-apologetic Early was battle-hardened, and clearly in charge. His new prestige as a division commander made Old Jube no less bad-tempered or mean.

During the action at Chancellorsville in May 1863, Early found himself in the shaky position of holding, with his lone division, the complete Fredericksburg line that Lee's entire army had occupied the previous December. Although Barksdale's brigade augmented him, the precarious assignment indicated that General Lee considered Early the division commander he most trusted with an independent command.

Hampered by confusion in orders, the 23,000-man Union Sixth Corps overran Early's men. But Old Jube kept his head while he withdrew. In the final stage of the battle, Early reoccupied the lost ground and counterattacked the Federals. That movement ended the Union threat, driving the Union Sixth Corps back across the river.

Everybody respected him for what he had accomplished militarily in the past two years. It was just that no one liked him.

General Early was known to be abusive to his subordinates, snarling at them like a cougar while issuing orders and directions. He was obnoxious with everyone. Constantly talking, the opinionated Virginian was dogmatic, persistent, and willing to take chances. He was overbearing with his peers.

General Early was a tall man, standing 6' in height, but had a slight but noticeable stoop, caused by inflamed rheumatism that he contracted while he was served in Mexico[2]. Although educated, his spoken words were usually grammatically incorrect, rough, coarse, and often profane. Balding, his dark straight hair flowed from under his gray brimmed hat. General Early himself would years later describe his "hair as straight as an Indian's and his eyebrows as moderate and smooth." General Early chewed tobacco, and had a most annoying habit of switching his quid from one side to the other, especially when he was excited. What a sight it was to see dark tobacco spit fly as General Early, the for-

---

[2] Jubal A. Early, Lieutenant General Jubal Anderson Early C. S. A. Autobiographical Sketch and Narrative of The War Between The States, with Notes by R. H. Early. J. B. Lippincott Company, Philadelphia & London, 1912. Page 26.

ever non-stop talker, excitedly spew words, orders, and profanities to everyone.

With his black eyes, piercing as ever, he watched everyone and everything, missing nothing, as he jabbered and sprayed spittle constantly. What sight this bent over tall man on the horse created wherever he went. Known for his self-reliance, Early "was an able strategist and one of the coolest and most imperturbable of men under fire and in extremity," according to fellow Confederate General John B. Gordon, who served as his subordinate.[3]

General Early's roughness caused one of his Federal prisoners to observe, there were many Confederates who would shoot him "just as quick as they would a damned Yankee."

Old Jube said what he meant, and he meant what he said, without exception. A true disciplinarian, General Early was so strict it seemed mere vindictiveness. Once when one of his regiments failed to protect a wagon train to his satisfaction, he galloped to his men and hissed and sprayed spit and words that he would put the regiment on the front line "where he hoped every one of them would get killed and burn through all eternity!"

General Early did exactly what he promised, and the army unit was decimated. Sending his men to hell, General Early was still admired by one of the unit's survivors. He later wrote that General Early was "a queer fish ... but no humbug."[4]

General Early often grumbled. Fanny Haralson Gordon, the pretty wife of one of General Early's commanders, frequently accompanied her husband, General John B. Gordon, on his military campaigns. For whatever reason, Fanny Gordon annoyed Old Jube. An officer overheard the bristling Early wishing to God that the Federals would soon capture her.[5]

---

[3] John B. Gordon, Reminiscences of The Civil War (New York: Scribner's, 1903), 317.

[4] Larry Tagg, The Generals of Gettysburg: The Leaders of America's Greatest Battle (El Dorado Hills, CA: Savas Publishing, 1998), 202.

[5] General Gordon recalls this story on Page 319 of his book. He said, "Mrs. Gordon was one of the few who were able to consult their wishes in this regard. General Early, hearing of her constant presence, is said to have exclaimed, "I wish the Yankees would capture Mrs. Gordon and hold her till the war is over!" Near Winchester, as the wagon-trains

Early did not like women traveling with his army, or even visiting. A life-long bachelor, Early stirred up the resentments of his men when he petitioned Major General Thomas "Stonewall" Jackson to order all the visiting wives, mothers, and sisters to stay away, citing them as an interruption in the army's work. General Jackson read General Early's letter and growled, "I will do no such thing. I wish my wife could come to see me!"

Except for the distance, and the Pennsylvania geography that included steep climbs and rolling hills, the long march was so far proving to be an easy one for the Southerners. There was no real Federal resistance. General Early and his Confederate Army had not seen a single blue coat in defense of the Commonwealth of Pennsylvania[6]. The Confederate Army moved as it wanted, going where it pleased, and so far was unchallenged in the Keystone State.

The day before, General Early's division had crossed the Potomac River at Shepherdstown, and moved on to Sharpsburg, Maryland. From there, he proceeded to Boonsborough. He had setup his camp that night on the road toward Hagerstown, about 3 miles from Boonsborough. Major General Ewell dispatched the 17th Virginia Cavalry, under Colonel William H. French to report

---

were being parked at night, he discovered a conveyance unlike any of the others that were going into camp. He immediately called out to his quartermaster in excited tones: "What 's that?" "That is Mrs. Gordon's carriage, sir," replied the officer. "Well, I 'll be - - - - -! If my men would keep up as she does, I 'd never issue another order against straggling." Mrs. Gordon was fully aware of the general's sentiments, and had heard of his wishing for her capture; and during a camp dinner given in honor of General Ewell, she sat near General Early and good-naturedly rallied him about it. He was momentarily embarrassed, but rose to the occasion and replied: "Mrs. Gordon, General Gordon is a better soldier when you are close by him than when you are away, and so hereafter, when I issue orders that officers' wives must go to the rear, you may know that you are excepted." This gallant reply called forth a round of applause from the officers at table."
[6] Other elements of the Confederate Army, such as those of General A. G. Jenkins, were skirmishing with the NY Cavalry.

to General Early. The troopers of the 17th Virginia Cavalry rested their horses in the Pennsylvania farm pastures.

The long day of marching was nearly over. The Confederates had marched through Cavetown, Smithtown, and Ringgold. It had been a good day's work. For the tired, weary, and thirsty soldiers, it felt good to rest in their makeshift encampment. General Early was satisfied with the progress his men made that day.

The Confederates setup their camp near Waynesborough[7], located just inside the Pennsylvania-Maryland border. The Southerners acquired food and supplies from the locals, paying for their acquisitions with Confederate dollars or Confederate army requisitions. To their east was South Mountain. And beyond that, there were Harrisburg and Philadelphia, and all the riches of many communities in between. General Lee soon would turn this part of his massive force of Southerners to cross South Mountain. Already, General Lee started the movement, ordering spearhead movements of some strong units of his overall force, over South Mountain.

General Early's mind must have been busy that night, when he finally laid his head on a pillow that summer night. So far, so good, but Jube Early knew there was so much more to do here in Pennsylvania.

Confederate General Jubal Early spent his second day in Pennsylvania breaking camp, and moving his army further north. It was another day that the Confederates had not seen a single Federal soldier defending the Commonwealth. The movement of Early's Confederate division remained unchecked as he marched his men through Quincy, past Altodale[8], and onto the pike that connected Gettysburg and Chambersburg. Just east of Fayetteville, in the small crossroads village of Greenwood, General Early decided to set up camp.

His army had moved about 12 miles this 24th day of June, on the western side of South Mountain. It was another good day's march for his men. The thick mountainous terrain, along with the summer warmth, tired the men and the horses. It was enough for

---

[7] Now known as Waynesboro.
[8] Now known as Mount Alto.

everyone. They earned and deserved the rest. It was an uneventful day for the thousands of Confederate soldiers under General Early's command.

Although General Early and his men were now moving deeper into Pennsylvania, it was not the first time the Southerners had invaded Pennsylvania. The previous October, Pennsylvania was invaded briefly when the Confederates raided Chambersburg.

It was a lightening raid and a quick strike, acquire, and run campaign.

Confederate General J.E.B. Stuart and his cavalry force of 1,800 men dashed north, through western Maryland, crossed the Mason-Dixon Line, and continued north to Chambersburg. When Stuart raided the town, his primary target was a Federal supply house.

When General Stuart charged into Chambersburg, he was under explicit orders from his commander, General Robert E. Lee. Stuart was ordered by Lee to treat all citizens, including those who would be taken hostage, "with all the respect and consideration that circumstances will admit."

Lee made his directive quite clear. His order defined for the invading forces what they were allowed to take: "Should it be in your power to supply yourself with horses, or other necessary articles on the list of legal capture, you are authorized to do so."

It was published in the *Valley Spirit*, November 5, 1862, with the headline, "The Invasion of Pennsylvania."[9]

It is interesting to note that General Lee authorized the capture of Pennsylvanians holding government positions. The newspaper published General Lee's order to General Stuart: Gen. Lee's Instructions.

---

[9] Page 1 column 3

HEADQUARTERS, ARMY of NORTHERN VA., Maj. Gen. J. E. B. Stuart, Commanding Cavalry:

General--An expedition into Maryland with a detachment of cavalry, if it can be successfully executed, is at this time desirable. You will, therefore, for a detachment of from twelve to fifteen hundred well mounted men, suitable for such an expedition, and should the information from your scouts lead you to suppose that your movement can be concealed from bodies of the enemy that would be able to resist it, you are desired to cross the Potomac above Williamsport, leave Hagerstown and Greencastle on your right, and proceed to the rear of Chambersburg, and endeavor to destroy the railroad bridge over the branch of the Conococheagne. Any other damage that you can inflict upon the enemy or his means of transportation you will also execute. You are desired to gain all information of the position, force and probable intent of the enemy which you can, and in your progress into Pennsylvania you will take measures to inform yourself of the various routes that you may take on your return to Virginia. To keep your movement secret it will be necessary for you to arrest all citizens that may give information to the enemy; and should you meet with citizens of Pennsylvania holding State or government offices, it will be desirable, if convenient, to bring them with you, that they may be used as hostages, or the means of exchange for our own citizens that have been carried off by the enemy. Such persons will, of course, be treated with all the respect and consideration that circumstances will admit. Should it be in your power to supply yourself with horses, or other necessary articles on the list of legal capture, you are authorised to do so. Having accomplished your errand you will rejoin this army as soon as practicable. Reliance is placed upon your skill and judgment in the successful execution of this plan, and it is not intended or desired that you should jeopardize the safety of your command, or go farther than your good judgment and prudence may dictate. Colonel Imboden has been desired to attract the attention of the enemy towards Cumberland, so that the river between that point and where you may recross may be less guarded. You will, of course, keep out your scouts to give you information, and take every other precaution to secure the success and safety of the expedi-

tion. Should you be led so far east as to make it better in your opinion, to continue around to the Potomac, you will have to cross the river in the vicinity of Leesburg.
I am, with great respect, your ob't serv't.
R. E. Lee, General.
Official: R. H. Chilton, A. A. General.

It was clear that General Robert E. Lee did not want to damage or destroy private property, for the sole purpose of simply destroying it because he could. Lee's orders clearly stated the boundaries of "legal capture." Lee did not want his men to violate the respect of the people of Chambersburg.

General Stuart followed Lee's orders, and added to them, in the orders that he gave to his troops. Stuart's orders stated explicitly, "Individual plunder for private use is positively forbidden, and in every instance must be punished in the severest manner, for an army of plunderers consummates its own destruction."

Stuart directed his subordinates to make it clear to their troops that the town of Chambersburg was not to be made into a battlefield. He directed that his troops understand that Pennsylvania's citizens were not to be treated as if they were enemy soldiers. Their property and their dignity were to be respected.

General Stuart's fast raid proved successful. They destroyed $250,000 of railroad property. His Confederates captured $150,000 worth of Federal supplies. His men took 1,200 horses and 500 guns, and burned the Federal storehouse. Everything taken was in the name of "legal capture."

Pennsylvania resident William Heyser, a shopkeeper located on the south side of Chambersburg, maintained a diary[10]. His entries describe the behavior and actions of the Confederates during their raid. The sixty-six year old Heyser made the following notation for October 10, 1862:

"Rain today. A great saving for the farmers who were facing a great drought. Business is flourishing in town. The Rebels are in Mercersburg, and on the way to Chambersburg from St. Thomas. This evening they entered our town, demanding its surrender.

---

[10] The Diary of William Heyser is located in the University of Virginia Library.

Some 1500-2000 cavalry, with some artillery. They immediately took possession of the bank and telegraph office. Also requisitioned provisions, clothing, etc. as to their needs. It has all happened so quickly, we all felt safe knowing the Union Army was in Williamsport, MD. The Confederate troops all look well fed and clothed, and so far, conducted themselves orderly. They will be busy stripping our stores and gathering up horses. I have sent my three off with Proctor, I hope they got away safely. I did not go to bed until after one o'clock, watching what may happen after all retire. So far, all quiet. Secreted some of my most valuable papers and went to bed, slept soundly until morning."

The following day, Heyser wrote more in his diary. His entries indicate that Stuart and his men obeyed Lee's orders.

"Clear and pleasant. Rose early and to the square. Saw Major Gen. Stewart and Gen. Hampden in conference. The stores were all closed. Broke open Isaac Hutton's shoe store, helped themselves freely. Then to the depot and confiscated a large shipment of arms and clothes. Afterwards, set fire to all the buildings and left town by the Baltimore Pike. They had fired the building of Wanderlick and Nead Co. which was used as a storehouse for government ammunition. The succeeding explosions of shells and powder was tremendous. The loss must be very great. All the machinery and present locomotives destroyed at the shops. This was all the fault of A.H. Lule, Supt. of the railroad shops. He should have sent the war supplies back to Carlisle, instead of keeping them here, being warned as early as three o'clock the past afternoon. However, this saved our stores from being pillaged as they got enough at the depot. Everybody out on the streets seeking news."

"About mid-day, a large scouting party of our troops came thru producing a great sensation. We hear of another group at Waynesboro, marching towards Gettysburg hoping to head them off. All in all the invasion was a very orderly one. The troops were well disciplined and polite. Not a single house or person injured. They were more orderly than troops of ours that have passed this way. Outside of their plundering of Isaac Hutton's shoe store, nothing else occurred to criticize them. Many people from the country came into town in search of news and carried home relics of the Rebel Invasion, as shells, balls, saber parts, parts of musquets , etc. Nearly every man and boy had some souvenir."

For the first Confederate invasion into Pennsylvania, the Southerners were disciplined and well behaved. Of course, they were led by General Stuart, and not General Early.

And everyone knew exactly what kind of man General Early was.

Confederate General Jubal Early. This photo was taken while he served in the Southern Army.

Jubal Early, as he looked around the time of his death.

Chapter 2
The Pennsylvania Emergency

On Wednesday, June 24, 1863, Confederate General Jubal Early and his force of Southerners were about 60 miles west of Wrightsville. It was a small town, located on the western shore of the Susquehanna River. About twenty miles north of the Mason-Dixon Line, Wrightsville was in York County. Directly across from Wrightsville, a little more than a mile away in Lancaster County, was the busy borough of Columbia.

Following the Southern victory at Chancellorsville in May, the U.S. War Department had notified the northern Governors of the likelihood of an invasion. Pennsylvania Governor Andrew Curtin, an unapologetic supporter of President Abraham Lincoln and the Union, was clearly concerned.

Curtin, a former Whig, had joined the new Republican Party in 1860. A lawyer from Bellefonte, Andrew Curtin never wavered with his support for Lincoln. Governor Curtin sensed the threat of an invasion real, and Pennsylvania was most likely the first northern state that the Southerners would invade.

In early June, the War Department divided Pennsylvania in half, creating two military departments. On June 9, the western half of the state became the Department of Monongahela, and the following day, Major General W. T. H. Brooks became its commander. The War Department also created the Department of Susquehanna on June 9, and issued orders of June 10 placing Major General Darius N. Couch in charge. President Lincoln personally approved the orders[11].

---

[11] United States War Department. The War of the Rebellion: a Compilation of the Official Records of the Union and Confederate Armies, 1880-1891. Chapter XXXIX, Part III, Page 55.

Although General Early's invasion into the Commonwealth of Pennsylvania had so far been unchallenged, it was most certainly not unnoticed. Reports of the Confederates in Pennsylvania flooded the office of the new commander of the Department of the Susquehanna. General Couch's Harrisburg headquarters was full of activity. General Couch scurried about, trying to assemble troops to defend Pennsylvania and the other northern states from the southern invasion.

He also worried.

General Couch knew first hand the strength of the Southern army and its destructive capability. He witnessed their force and might a month earlier at Chancellorsville. At that four-day battle, the Confederates proved they could use strategy to overcome a much superior sized Federal army. The Confederate Generals, with their force of about 60,000 men, out maneuvered the Federal Generals, whose force numbered about 130,000 men. The truth was that at the Battle of Chancellorsville the Confederates proved they had the skill to overtake and decimate a force twice their size.

General Couch was a veteran commander in the Army of the Potomac. A native of South East, a small town in located just inside the New York-Connecticut border west of Danbury, Couch graduated from West Point in 1846. Couch served in the Mexican War with the 4th Artillery at Buena Vista. He then served against the Seminoles. In 1853, while on leave from the military, Couch went on an expedition for the Smithsonian Institution into Mexico. There the military man gained distinction for as a naturalist, and discovered a new bird, the Tyrannus couchii. This little gray and yellow bird was named after its discoverer[12]. By 1855, Couch had drifted out of the army, and became a merchant in New York and a manufacturer in Massachusetts. When the Civil War started, Couch joined the 7th Massachusetts as a colonel. The army quickly promoted Couch to brigadier general. When his second star was added to his shoulder, he found himself serving at the Battle of Fredericksburg in 1862. Couch was the II Corps Commander at Chancellorsville in May, 1863.

Couch had asked for a leave of absence, reportedly telling his seniors that he could not longer lead his men to "senseless slaugh-

---

[12] It is still known today as the Couch Kingbird.

ter" under General Joe Hooker. General Couch was also suffering from ill health. Instead of granting his leave request, the War Department reassigned the tough and aggressive Couch to the newly established Department of the Susquehanna as its commander. He had only a small number of troops when he took command of the recently constituted department. His primary job was to oversee a fledgling new Pennsylvania militia. Couch, using his authority, issued orders for volunteers to enlist in the state's defense. He brought vast military experience to the post. The creation of the Department of the Susquehanna was designed to facilitate the military regional movements and activities within the area. As the department's new commander, General Couch controlled all military within his designated area.

Governor Curtin quickly followed Couch's lead. On June 12, Curtin issued a proclamation calling for "able bodied men to volunteer for military service in "emergency" militia regiments."

"Information has been obtained by the War Department that a large rebel force, composed of cavalry, artillery, and mounted infantry, has been prepared for the purpose of making a raid into Pennsylvania," Governor Curtin had said[13].

General Couch added, "To prevent serious raids by the enemy, it is deemed necessary to call upon the citizens of Pennsylvania, to furnish promptly, all the men necessary to organize an army corps of volunteer infantry, cavalry, and artillery, to be designated the Army Corps of the Susquehanna. It was announced that the troops so organized, were intended for service in these two Departments, but that they would "be mustered into the service of the United States, to serve during the pleasure of the President, or the continuance of the war."

Men were desperately needed to defend the state's soil. General Couch was ready to accept any able-bodied men from 18 to 60 years old into his army of defenders.

General Couch realized that he had less than 300 men that had been properly armed and organized to defend the Commonwealth of Pennsylvania. General Lee probably knew that too, from a network of spies and southern sympathizers, commonly

---

[13] Samuel P. Bates, Martial Deeds of Pennsylvania (Philadelphia: T. H. Davis & Co., 1876), 168.

called copperheads. Pennsylvania seemed like easy pickings for Confederates.

As summer arrived, there was a flurry of activity in the Pennsylvania's capital. A newly bearded General Couch planned for the defense of the Harrisburg. An experienced and trained military man, Couch realized that Pennsylvania's capital was a likely target of an invading Confederate force. Because of its location, cutting it off from Philadelphia and Baltimore would create havoc to the Union. It had, over the past decade, become a major hub for the railroad, moving supplies and men for the Union army in east and west, and north and south. Camp Curtin was the Union's largest training camp, and it included a large depot of supplies. If the Confederates captured the supplies, it would help their cause. Even if the Federals destroyed the depot to prevent the materials from falling into the hands of the Confederates, it was worthwhile. South central Pennsylvania had an abundance of farms, capable of producing food for the Confederate army. Nearby manufacturing was desperately needed by the Southerners. Factories produced clothing and metal objects.

Moreover, most importantly, Harrisburg was a northern state capital. President Lincoln would not have been just embarrassed, but humiliated and powerless if the Southerners captured Harrisburg. It would turn the Union against him, the Southerners project had theorized. The Confederates also presumed that if they captured a northern capital, it was likely to impress the European nations. That could lead to securing aid, or recognition of the Confederate States of America. Harrisburg was simply too tempting a target for a force of invading Southerners to ignore.

And General Couch knew it, too. He could read a map.

On June 14, volunteers consisting of local citizens began digging trenches around the state capital. The work was difficult, backbreaking, and nearly impossible. Just few inches under the surface, hard shale tired the citizen workers. By the end of the day, they gave up.

The next day, the work resumed. But this time the strong backs of African-American railroad construction crews were pressed into service. The free Blacks feverishly broke through the hardened shale. They were paid 75 cents per day for their exhausting and demanding labor. The primary site for the earthen defenses was Hummel Hill[14]. It was located on the western end of the Camelback Bridge. It soon became known as Fort Washington, and sprawled across about 60 acres. Twenty-five pieces of field artillery, mounted behind the earthen redoubts on wooden platforms, soon defended the fort. Troops from the New York militia were assigned to the fort for the city's protection.

Living in tents, the men drank water from barrels filled from water from the Susquehanna. A local volunteer fire company pumped the water up the hill.

Slightly to the south of the present-day Market Street Bridge on the west shore of the Susquehanna, Lemoyne was the site of Fort Couch. Another defensive position, it was positioned to protect the larger Fort Washington location. Here again, black Americans from the railroad construction crews provided the hard labor needed to dig ditches for the defense of the capital city.

Major General Couch hurriedly and persistently continued his work. Issuing orders, preparing defenses, and assembling the green volunteers of the newly forming Pennsylvania militia, General Couch had plenty to do, and little time to do it.

On June 15, 1863, Special Orders No. 3 was issued at the Headquarters of the Department of the Susquehanna. Under the signature of Jno. S. Schultze, Captain and Acting Adjutant-General, V. Captain C.C. Haldeman was "authorized to raise troops, and assume command of the same, for the Defense of Columbia, and the bridges, dams, and fords on the Susquehanna River in the vicinity.[15] It is clear from this order – one of the earliest from the newly formed Department of the Susquehanna, the strategic importance of the Columbia-Wrightsville Bridge weighed heavily on General Couch's mind.

He had only been placed in command five days earlier. It was only his fourth day in Harrisburg.

Early that same day, General Couch assessed the situation, from a military point of view, and sent a message to the U.S. Secretary of War. At 9:12 a. m., he wrote, "All is being done that is in our power to resist the invasion, but, as matters look now, all

---

[14] Today, this area is known as Washington Heights.
[15] The order identifies V. Captain C.C. Haldeman of Columbia County. Most likely, it should have read C.C. Haldeman, Columbia, of Lancaster County.

south of the Susquehanna will be swept. Orders are being sent north to run out all horses, &c."[16]

On June 15, 1863, President Abraham Lincoln called for 100,000 men from Pennsylvania, West Virginia, Ohio, and Maryland. These men were to serve for a period of six months or as long as necessary during the present emergency. Lincoln's proclamation for the volunteers added an extra military force for the United States. In his proclamation, he called for 50,000 volunteers specifically from the Commonwealth of Pennsylvania. Lincoln's proclamation said the volunteers were "to be mustered into the service of the United States forthwith and to serve for the period of six months from the date of such muster into said service, unless sooner discharged; to be mustered in as infantry, artillery and cavalry, in proportions which will be made known through the War Department, which Department will also designate the several places of rendezvous."

The looming emergency was hurriedly mounting. The armed rebellion was threatening. Many military age Pennsylvanians ignored the call to service. The President's, Governor's, and General Couch's call for troops proved wretchedly ineffectual. Among the Pennsylvania population, there was apathy.

General Couch had learned on this day that his pickets – located about nine miles south of Chambersburg, were already spotting advancing Confederates.

It did not take long for General Couch to realize the importance of the grand covered bridge that linked York and Lancaster Counties across the Susquehanna. General Couch requested that the citizens along the river to organize emergency men to keep watch for the approach of the Confederates, and he directed a committee from Columbia to visit him at Harrisburg.

---

[16] United States War Department. The War of the Rebellion: a Compilation of the Official Records of the Union and Confederate Armies, 1880-1891. Chapter XXXIX, Part III, Page 129.

"I was one of the committee that went up to see him (General Couch), and he impressed us with the necessity of keeping a sharp lookout for any advance of the Confederates to this point, as he did at other points along the Susquehanna River," George W. Haldeman of Columbia said. "Among other things that he requested was that the citizens should watch for the approach of the Confederates by way of York…"[17]

At 8 p.m. on June 16, 1863, General Couch sent a telegraph to the Secretary of War. A Confederate deserter, who was a Northern Irishman, told the Federals that Confederate General J.E.B. Stuart had orders read to his men that said they would reach Philadelphia before their return to the south.

"The country is so wild with rumors that I was compelled to use great caution in communicating with you," General Couch said. "I have made every exertion to protect the bridges across the Susquehanna, but they are to be fired, if it becomes necessary."[18]

U.S. Secretary of War Edwin M. Stanton inquired if General Couch had sufficient power to carry about his duties. On June 20, 1863, at 3:00 p.m., Secretary Stanton telegraphed a message to General Couch, asking as "to the powers granted are as large and discretionary as you desire in the present emergency, or whether other and what power is needed?" Secretary Stanton asked for an immediate answer.

General Couch responded within 65 minutes. He wrote, "My powers are ample. I require nothing more."[19]

---

[17] From a sworn deposition taken from George W. Haldeman on August 19, 1904 in Columbia, PA.

[18] United States War Department. The War of the Rebellion: a Compilation of the Official Records of the Union and Confederate Armies, 1880-1891. Chapter XXXIX, Part III, Page 163.

[19] United States War Department. The War of the Rebellion: a Compilation of the Official Records of the Union and Confederate Armies, 1880-1891. Chapter XXXIX, Part III, Page 240.

Confederate General Jubal Early was, on June 24, only about 50 miles southwest of Harrisburg.

It was clear now that the Union had to brace for the greatest threat it had known since declaring independence from Britain. The defense of the northern states, particularly Pennsylvania, weighed heavily on President Lincoln, his War Department, and the commanders of the Army of the Potomac.

On the day that General Early and his force of invading Southerners bivouacked near Fayetteville, lots of activity continued in Harrisburg. The threat of the southern invasion was now a reality. As the constant call for volunteers united native Pennsylvanians, a determined group of sixteen rallied to the call. While many sat on the sidelines, ignoring the Governor and President's call for volunteers, others were stirred into action. One such event occurred in Harrisburg. On June 24, 1863, a Harrisburg correspondent of the Philadelphia *Press*, described the scene when a special company of Pennsylvania volunteers appeared in town.

> *"I was just about to commence this letter, when I heard the sound of a drum and fife. Looking out of the window, I saw a small company of men marching up the street, and bearing three colors; one, a small, worn, and tattered silk flag, and the others new and fresh. As they approached nearer, I discovered that they were very old men, and my curiosity being excited, I ran out and followed them to the Capitol, whither they were marching. And here is what I learned: They were sixteen in all, members of the Soldiers' Association of 1812, of Harrisburg. The oldest was seventy-six, and the youngest sixty-eight. Every man had served in the war of 1812, and all belonged to a regiment commanded by General Foster, who has lately died, and who is remembered with respect and affection as one of the best citizens of this county. They were reviewed by General Scott, at Baltimore, after he was wounded. He rode up and down the ranks with his arm in a sling. The tattered flag was borne by a Pennsylvania regiment, at the battle of Trenton, in 1777, and has been cherished in Harrisburg ever since that time. These veterans marched up to the Governors room, and tendered their services*

for the emergency. They wished to be put behind entrenchments, but, if any other and harder service was required of them, they would cheerfully attempt it. In a few appropriate words, they addressed the Governor, and he accepted them. The only favor they asked, was to be armed with the old flint-lock muskets, such as they used to carry when they were young.

It was a grand and inspiring sight! Those old men, scarcely hoping to live through the war, their locks white with the frosts of many winters, their frames bowed by age, and long toil in the journey of life, marched as briskly and accurately to the drum and fife, as any of their grandsons could. They seemed almost carried back to the olden time, so inspiriting was the occasion. When they came out of the Governor's room, they marched, according to the old fashion, in single file. They were halted on the green. It was curious to modern ears to hear the orders of the Captain — so different from our tactics. It was: 'by sections of two, march;' instead of 'file right,' or 'left,' it was 'right,' or 'left wheel;' instead of the sharp, short, peremptory 'front,' it was 'left face.' So they marched down in the town, carrying the old tactics of the revolution with them. They kept their places, and kept step and obeyed orders with a precision that showed that the drill they had gone through in those stirring times, had gone not merely to the ear, but to the heart. Wherever they passed a squad of soldiers, they were loudly cheered—' three cheers for the veterans of 1812!' and such lusty shouts as split the heavens, you never heard. They were observed by every one, and some would ask who they were. The bowed forms, the gray heads, and the small, torn and decayed ensign, told the whole story.

What an example to the young men of Harrisburg! I cannot put the point more forcibly than by quoting a rather irreverent expression of a young Pennsylvania soldier, who, after his two years' service had expired, volunteered again at this crisis. He said, as he surveyed them drawn up in line, "It is rather hard on you old cocks to have to come out. This ---- neighborhood has sent sixty men — and here are sixteen old men, with one foot in the grave, ready to volunteer." Comment is unnecessary.

I took pains to inquire their names, and, for curiosity, their politics. There are thirteen Republicans, descended from all parties — Federalist, Whig, and Democratic — and three Democrats. I hope I shall not trespass on your space by giving their names. They ought to be written in letters of gold. They ought to be posted on every corner of Harrisburg.

The names are as follows: C. Carson, Captain; Andrew Krause, Lieutenant — (were in the battle of Lundy's Lane, and all through Scott's campaign) — J.R. Boyd, Wm. Bostwick, George Heiney, John Heisley, D. Harris, (secretary of the association;) S. Holman, A. Sturgeon, D.J. Krause, W.P. Brady, George McKnight, G. Cunkle, George Prince, John Shannon, George J. Heisley, Jacob Kuhn.

These old heroes will go into the rifle-pits, and fight as of yore, for liberty and the Union. What they mean they say; and their earnestness is proven by their asking for old flint-lock muskets, such as they were use to. Let the young men beware, or their grandsires will set them an example they will blush not to have forestalled. W."[20]

The descendants of those earlier American patriots now filled the ranks of the Pennsylvania volunteer troops. Camp Curtin, on the north side of the city of Harrisburg, filled with the newly arriving volunteer troops. Just a few blocks from the camp, the Susquehanna River flowed south. About 28 miles down river, people in the Lancaster County Borough of Columbia were just as full of activity as the citizens in the state capital.

In the second half of June 1863, life in the small borough of Columbia, Pennsylvania was as hectic as ever. It was always an industrious, bustling little community, ever since its early founding. Located on the western edge of Lancaster County, Columbia was on the eastern shore of the Susquehanna River.

---

[20] *The Press.* Philadelphia, PA. Friday, June 26, 1863 issue. Vol. 6 — No. 279. A copy of this article is preserved on microfilm and available at the Pennsylvania State Library, Harrisburg, PA.

It was a town with a long history. It was strategically located. It was established fifty years before Pennsylvania would unite with the other colonies to declare its independence from England.

For decades, traffic heading west from Lancaster, Philadelphia, and all points between routinely converged at Columbia. Fully loaded Conestoga Wagons stopped and waited in the river town. Pulled by a team of four or six horses, the boat shaped wagons were painted Persian blue. Their white canvas coverings looked like bonnets. Congestion caused by the movement of freight, goods, supplies, and people, often caused days of waiting. Columbia offered the travelers or teamsters food, taverns, and supplies. It was not uncommon for 150 to 200 vehicles waiting for "their turn" to cross the Susquehanna. The ferrymen used chalk to number the vehicles.[21]

In the early years, the wagons waited for an opportunity to cross the Susquehanna River on a flatboat ferry. Crossing the Susquehanna required time.

From what is now Maryland, in the northeast corner of the Chesapeake Bay, the mighty and forceful Susquehanna River extends due north some 444 miles. It slices directly through Pennsylvania, and extends into central New York State, where it rises from its meek beginnings. The river flows south, constantly gaining in size and volume, as tributaries and creeks feed it along the way. The river grows in volume and strength. The water flows out of Pennsylvania a short distance into Maryland, and once there, fills the great Chesapeake Bay.

Long before the arrival of William Penn and his fellow European settlers, native people lived along the river's fertile shores. Known as Susquehannocks, their native villages were simple. They relied on the Susquehanna River as a main source for their food. Living in the general area of what is today Columbia, the Native Americans recognized the value of the location. With its gentle hills, the soil is rich with limestone. It is some of the most productive farmland found throughout North America.

Speaking Iroquois, these tough spirited native people probably migrated from what is now New York. They traveled along

---

[21] Franklin Ellis and Samuel Evans. History of Lancaster County, Pennsylvania with Biographical Sketches of Many of Its Pioneers and Prominent Men. (Philadelphia: Everts & Peck, 1883). Page 540.

the Susquehanna River, and established a colony just south of modern day Columbia. The Susquehannocks migrated into the area probably around 1575 to 1600. They had separated from the Iroquois, a federation of the Mohawk, Oneida, Cayuga, Seneca, and Onondaga.

It was in 1608 that Europeans explorers first noted the existence of the Susquehannocks. None other than Captain John Smith, the legendary friend of Pocahontas, while exploring the Chesapeake Bay and lower Susquehanna River, encountered the Native Americans. He described them as "giants[22]."

Captain Smith was directly responsible for naming these native people. Susquehannock, as well as the name for the Susquehanna River, derives from the word Sasquesahanough, a descriptive word used by Smith's Algonquian interpreter. The translated word meant People at the Falls, or People of the Muddy River. It was from that interpreter's lips that Smith forever named those native people and that grand river.

In a small place, tucked along the Susquehanna River, close to what today is known as Washington Boro, this breakaway group of Native Americans stopped their migration south and set up their village. Others established villages further south along the Susquehanna, continuing further south into modern day Maryland.

The Susquehannocks constructed stockade-type villages and lived in multi-family longhouses, measuring between 60 to 80 feet in length. The Susquehannock society was matriarchal[23].

The Susquehannocks were an advancing people and great traders. The location of their lower Susquehanna home put them in close proximity to the newly arriving European traders on the Delaware and Chesapeake bays. Smith had estimated their population to be about 2,000 at the time of his visit. Within the next

---

[22] Their graves, studied centuries later by archeologists, reveals nothing to indicate they were abnormally large.

[23] The term means these early American Indians traced their descent through their mother. The married men of the village lived with their wives' families.

150 years, the lives of the descendants of the Susquehannocks John Smith had discovered would vastly change.

Throughout the 1600's, the Susquehannocks formed alliances with other Native Americans, and waged war with other tribes and the European settlers, all in an effort to maintain control of their land and the commerce that was developing. The Susquehannocks had always been allies of the Huron and enemies of the Iroquois.

They brutally fought with the Delaware to the east, the Mohawk to the north, and the Powhatan to the south. Besides trying to maintain control of their native land and its natural trading routes, the Susquehannocks fought for the profits from business with the European fur traders. They wanted the European's manufactured products, including their firearms. The Susquehannocks were the only Native American tribe that established friendly relations with all the newly arriving Europeans: the French, the Dutch, the Swedes, and the English. The Susquehannocks had signed treaties with the colonial governors of New York, Pennsylvania, Maryland, and Virginia. From their main village, they spread out, in both directions, up and down along the Susquehanna.

The Susquehannocks paid a heavy toll for their warring. Many of their young warriors died in battles. Disease, particularly small pox, devastated their riverside communities. Their social structure began to fail with their declining numbers. By the end of the 1600's, only a few hundred Susquehannocks remained as an identifiable tribe within Pennsylvania. They migrated as far away as Virginia, but later returned to their ancestral home to build a new village. Conestoga Town was the name of their new settlement.

The Conestoga was the latest and last name of these existing Susquehannocks. Located south of modern day Lancaster City, the Conestoga established their Conestoga Town along the Conestoga River, which flows to the Susquehanna. Americans remember the name of the Indian town, not because of their descendency from the Susquehannocks, but because of a rugged and functional wagon that developed near it by future Pennsylvanians. Years later, the Conestoga wagon offered a means of reliable transportation. Perhaps ironically, so many of those wagons waited to cross the Susquehanna just north of the area where the people lived whose name described this transportation vehicle.

It was a period of great change in the Susquehannock's native land. An ocean away, in 1681, William Penn had petitioned Charles II, the King of England, for a grant of land in America to repay a debt owed to the Penn family. King Charles likely agreed to Penn's requests as a step towards removing the bothersome and annoying Quakers from England. Penn's charter established the boundaries of the new colony in American, named Penn as Proprietor with the right to dispose of the land and write laws for its inhabitants. The English King conferred the name Pennsylvania ("Penns Woods") upon the granted land in honor of English Admiral Sir William Penn.

When William Penn arrived in America, he set about establishing Philadelphia and the immediate surrounding area. Initially little concern was paid the western frontier, which was at that time, the lands of modern day Lancaster County. The first European settlers to live in the Susquehannock territory in this part of the New World were fur traders. William Penn deeded land in what is now Lancaster County to John Kennerly in 1691. He was the first established settler, and it took just 10 years from the time King Charles granted Penn the land until settlers were encroaching the Susquehannock's land, moving ever closer to the Susquehanna River.

In 1710, a group of Mennonites established the first permanent settlement of "plain people" in Lancaster County. Fleeing from persecution in search of find religious freedom, they settled east of what is now the community of Willow Street located near the Conestoga Town. The bishop who led this group for freedom seekers was Hans Herr. His small home, built in 1719, remains the oldest building in the county. Some years later, the Amish, a more conservative group of Mennonites, arrived in the county.

William Penn established three original counties in his beloved Penn's Woods. Philadelphia, Bucks, and Chester Counties were the first counties, but the settlers pushed west, away from Philadelphia and closer to the Susquehanna River. Leaders of religious groups continued the push, and settled on the Susquehannocks' former lands. Settlers received grants of large blocks of land.

Conestoga Town was a real Native American village, complete with Pennsylvania Indians that were friendly with the European settlers. Conestoga Town became the central hub for trade for the settlers with the Indians. Together they lived in harmony under the protection of the provincial government of Pennsylvania. Maybe that is what attracted the politicians of the day. It was here in Conestoga Town that the Native Americans and the European's signed treaties. William Penn traveled from Philadelphia to Conestoga Town in 1700. There he signed a treaty, as did later Pennsylvania Governors. Quaker missionaries eventually converted the Conestoga to Christians.

In 1726, John Wright had traveled to the area. A Quaker, he decided to settle, and preach to the Indians that lived near the often-roaring river. Sometimes the river was low, and allowed the crossing at fords. Other times, the current was swift. The rocky bottom, with dangerous crevices, could swallow a man on the next step.

Wright settled on the western edge of what was then Chester County, along the great Susquehanna. He was at a spot where the river was a mile wide, an area once hunted by the Susquehannocks. It was a beautiful vista deep in Penn's Woods, some sixty miles west of Philadelphia. Wright recognized what the Susquehannocks learned decades earlier. It was a perfect location along the wide river.

European settlers continued their colonization of the New World. Along with Robert Barber and Samuel Blunston, John Wright started a ferry business to provide transportation across the wide river. It offered those settlers, heading west past the Susquehanna, an easy way to cross the flowing river.

Another nearby ferry, Cresap's Blue Rock Ferry, never gained in popularity. Located further south, it never garnered the same traffic as Wright's Ferry.

Wright petitioned Penn's son to create new county, and in 1729, the provincial government set up the fourth county in Pennsylvania. Penn named the county Lancaster, taking away land from Chester County to form the new county. Wright had requested the name, which was in honor of his home country of England.

Now the Susquehannock's old land had a new name. It filled with settlers. It was here, in the town known as Wright's Ferry, that residents of the newly established Lancaster County traveled to seek provincial government assistance and to register land deeds. In a Wright's house, Indians and colonists both appeared, to file claims and papers, seeking government redress of issues.

Commerce fueled growth. Some 12 miles away, the town of Lancaster became the county seat. Villages and hamlets grew throughout the rolling hills of the county. Industrious and hard working settlers, deeply religious, tilled the land and produced an abundance of crops. It was a changing area, and a changing time. Over fifty million feet of lumber moved through Columbia annually. Great quantities of produce arrived. Workers loaded the products on riverboats, destined for markets.[24]

For what was left of the descendants of the Susquehannocks, life was never the same. Their numbers dwindling, the Conestoga lived peacefully along the Conestoga River. The Conestoga survived as farmers and crafts persons.

In 1763, just one hundred years before Confederate General Jubal Early invaded Pennsylvania with his Southern division, it was the end of the Conestoga. Chief Pontiac of the Ottawa nation led uprisings against settlers in the Great Lakes region, which included western Pennsylvania. Although the Conestoga were peaceful farmers, artisans, and converted Christians, with no connection to the rebellion in the west, a group of vigilantes known as the Paxton Boys viciously attacked them.

The Paxton Boys lived in Paxton (Paxtang) Township near Harrisburg, then the western frontier of colonial Pennsylvania. They protested the colonial government's unwillingness to aid the western settlers against the Indians. Therefore, they simply took matters into their own hands. With a force numbering in the hundreds and armed primarily with hand weapons, the Paxton Boys stayed outside the English law and common decency for several years. Fed by a frenzy of reports of what the warriors loyal to Chief Pontiac were doing in western Pennsylvania, the

---

[24] William H. Egle, M.D. An Illustrated History of the Commonwealth of Pennsylvania, Civil, Political, and Military, From Its Earliest Settlement to the Present Time. (Harrisburg, PA: De Witt C. Goodrich & Co., 1876). Page 833.

Paxton Boys vowed revenge. This group of organized thugs, self-appointed militia, and protectors of the settlers found the Conestoga an easy target. The mounted Paxton Boys galloped into Conestoga Town, and quickly slaughtered the six people they found in the village. True to their word, they brutally killed any Indian they saw.

The provincial council of Lancaster County ordered the remaining Conestoga taken into protective custody. However, their plan failed. Authorities transported fourteen Conestoga – men, women, and children -- to the city jail, and locked them in for their own protection.

The Paxton Boys rode back into town, and like bloodhounds, found the Conestoga. They broke into the jail. There they did their dirty work, slaughtering all fourteen Conestoga, beating them to a bloody pulp. The blood-splattered Paxton Boys did not stop until all the Conestoga were dead. Not a single person challenged any of the Paxton Boys. Authorities never charged anyone with a crime. Although most colonists were appalled when they heard the news of what had happened, no one answered for the vicious attack that had occurred in Lancaster. There were never any legal consequences for anyone that participated in the massacre of the Conestoga[25].

At that point, only two Conestoga, a husband and wife known as Michael and Mary, survived the attack. Only because they had been away, working at another farm, they lived. Pennsylvania Governor John Penn eventually issued papers of protection, which remained in effect until their death. When Michael and Mary eventually died, it was the end of the Conestoga peoples[26].

---

[25] The actual location of the massacre is where the current Fulton Opera House is located on Prince Street, just north of King Street in Lancaster, PA.

[26] Final Census of the Conestoga, recorded by Lancaster County Sheriff John Hays, 1763.

Murdered at Conestoga Town:

Sheehays, Wa-a-shen (George), Tee-Kau-ley (Harry), Ess-canesh (son of Sheehays), Tea-wonsha-i-ong (an old woman), Kannenquas (a woman)

Murdered at the Lancaster Workhouse:

However, it was not the end of what their ancestors had started. For years, the area grew. Just north of Washington Borough, the now thriving town known as Columbia welcomed visitors and travelers daily. It had changed its name from Wright's Ferry in 1788, hoping to become the nation's capital.

Samuel Wright laid out additional plans for a town of 160 lots he had hoped to become the nation's capital. The lots were chanced off by a lottery and 40 new dwellings appeared by 1800, and the area became more diverse. Within a generation, freed African slaves, English Anglicans, German Lutherans, Scots-Irish Presbyterians, and descendants of French Huguenots outnumbered the descendants of the town's first Quaker settlers.

Just as the Susquehannocks realized two centuries earlier, it was an ideal geographic location. George Washington favored the spot to become the nation's capital. By one vote, Congress chose another site. Congress selected another location, south of Baltimore, carving the capital out of Maryland on the Potomac River.

Columbia prospered and was now a busy town filled with commerce. The beautiful scenery by the Susquehanna was a great attraction to early travelers. The sloping ground offered outstanding vistas. The slope was densely covered with a forest of hickory, oak, and chestnut trees.[27] The gentle slope between the hills north and south of Columbia almost seemed like an open door to the west.

In February 1826, the Pennsylvania state legislature had approved the expenditure of $300,000 for canal construction along the eastern short of the Susquehanna. On December 17, 1830, the first section connecting to the nearby Chickies Creek was com-

---

Kyunqueagoah (Captain John), Koweenasee (Betty, his wife), Tenseedaagua (Bill Sack), Kanianguas (Molly, his wife), Saquies-hat-tah (John Smith), Chee-na-wan (Peggy, his wife), Quaachow (Little John, Capt John's son), Shae-e-kah (Jacob, a boy), Ex-undas (Young Sheehays, a boy), Tong-quas (Chrisly, a boy), Hy-ye-naes (Little Peter, a boy), Koqoa-e-un-quas (Molly, a girl), Karen-do-uah (a little girl), Canu-kie-sung (Peggy, a girl)

Survivors on the farm of Christian Hershey:
Michael and Mary (his wife)

[27] H.M. J. Klein, Ph. D., Editor in Chief. Lancaster County Pennsylvania, A History. (New York: Lewis Historical Publishing Company Inc. 1924). Page 305

pleted. The canals provided transportation for goods until the railroads took over.

By 1863, it was a place where canals, railroads, and the pikes converged. The Northern Central Railway main line connected there. There were two railroad round houses. The Pennsylvania Railroad had its own YMCA in Columbia to provide overnight lodging for its train crews.

It also had a bridge.

It was a grand bridge, owned by the Columbia Bridge Company. It offered travelers safe and convenient travel across the wide Susquehanna River.

A bridge builder had completed the existing bridge in 1834. Construction had started two years earlier. It was the second bridge to be stretch across the Susquehanna between Columbia and Wrightsville.

In the early 1800's, it was common for up to 150 Conestoga Wagons to congregate in Columbia, waiting two or three days to be ferried across the Susquehanna. The owner of the ferry also happened to own the local tavern.[28]

Years before, when John Wright procured the charter for his ferry service, he erected a tavern on the north side of Locust Street. In 1730, Wright's tavern was built of logs, and was two stories in height. There was a large room on both ends, with a passageway between the two grand rooms. John Wright, Jr. kept the tavern, operating it until 1734, when he married, moved to present day Wrightsville. He opened a tavern in Wrightsville, and operated it.[29]

Times change, and the demands of a traveling and growing nation made the construction of a bridge economically feasible. Pennsylvania embarked on an era of turnpike and bridge building. To lessen the congestion and wait caused by the congested ferry line, the world's largest covered bridge was built. A newly formed Columbia Bank and Bridge Company underwrote the construction of the bridge. Contracts were awarded, and construction began in 1812. Built according to what was known as the "Burr Plan,' the first bridge opened in 1814. At a cost of $231,771 to

---

[28] Susan Q. Stranhan. Susquehanna River of Dreams. (Baltimore, The John Hopkins Press, 1993). 55.

build, the bridge handled the east-west traffic across the Susquehanna for 18 years. It had 54 stone peers, was 30 feet wide, and 5,690 feet long.

The bridge was covered, a practice that first started in Pennsylvania. The reason was simple: the sides and roof protected the bridge from the rain, ice, and snow. Preventing rot to the timbers and lumber prolonged the life of the bridge. At some point, these bridges became known as "kissing bridges." A beau traveling with his adoring girlfriend could lean over and steal a kiss, protected from prying eyes by the structure of the bridge. The bridges rattled when used, and their interiors were often whitewashed. Birds built their nests in the rafters, and sometimes an owl perched there, too. Openings were cut in the side to allow a view of the flowing water.

Ice and severe weather damaged the first bridge to span the Susquehanna between Columbia and Wrightsville on February 18, 1832. An enormous ice jam carried away five spans. An enormous ice gorge, about 40 feet high, formed below the bridge and backed the water and ice over Front Street in Columbia. The river filled with relentless ice. Within the next few days, the entire bridge lay in ruins along the Susquehanna's shores. That summer, they began work on the second bridge.

The new construction was a great covered bridge, and at the time, the longest ever built in America. It took $128,726 to build the second bridge. A grand structure, it consisted of 28 stone piers, and 2 stone abutments. The long bridge had a covered roof made of shingles to protect it from adverse weather. Its sides were covered with weatherboard. Workers had whitewashed the bridge's interior. People crossed the bridge on foot, horse, wagon, and carriage. The railroad also now used the bridge, as it had a double-track railway. There were two towpaths, used to guide canal boat traffic across the Susquehanna. The bridge was "28 feet wide, and 5,620 feet long, making 340 feet over a mile[30]."

In 1840, the Canal Company modified it at a cost of $90,000. Two towing paths were added onto the south side of the bridge. From these paths, teams of mules or horses pulled the canal boats

---

[30] The measurements of the bridge are taken from the sworn deposition of Joseph H. Black, which was taken on August 19, 1904, and part of the record of the Court of Claims, 10492, Page 5.

from the east or west shores of the Susquehanna. Carpenters ingeniously constructed the paths at differing levels. Their finished work featured a narrow roofed platform, and a low sidewall to prevent the towing horses from falling into the river. The roof of the lower path formed the floor of the path above. The side openings were quite large. At times of flood, the Susquehanna River's current grew rapid and swift. The force of the water often yanked or pulled the towing animals from the bridge paths, plunging them into the flowing river water. One such incident was reported in the *Wrightsville Star* in the year 1854. A canal boat, towed by one horse and a pair of mules, crossed the river during a flood stage. The newspaper reported that all three horses were pulled into the river. The horse drowned, but the mules made it by swimming to shore. Workers rescued the canal boat, which was close enough to shore, before it went over the canal dam.[31]

Railroad traffic started early in Columbia. Despite the abundance of the nearby timber, construction workers did not initially use wooden ties. To build the railroad, they used red sand stones, fixing the rails with iron spikes. On Monday, March 31, 1834, three passenger cars drawn by horses arrived in town. Just a few days later, on April 2, three cars pulled into Columbia under the power of a locomotive.[32]

The burgeoning railroad industry was a boon to Columbia's economy. On May 19, 1857, the Reading and Columbia Railroad was incorporated. On June 24, 1857, there was a public meeting in the old town hall to urge the town's residents of Columbia to subscribe for the stock and company. About $25,000 was raised at the meeting. James Myers, Samuel Shoch, J.G. Hess, William A. Martin, Amos E. Green, Hugh M. North, Samuel W. Mifflin, and H. M. Strickler, all of Columbia, were among the Reading and Columbia Railroad's incorporators.

---

[31] Wrightsville 1736-1976 – Gateway to the West. Published by the Wrightsville Bicentennial Committee in 1976. A copy is on file at the Columbia Public Library.

[32] H.M. J. Klein, Ph. D., Editor in Chief. Lancaster County Pennsylvania, A History. (New York: Lewis Historical Publishing Company Inc. 1924). Page 305

The railroad brought large quantities of iron ore, and furnaces were built. This attracted laborers to Columbia, increasing the town's population.

As a growing and essential railroad center, it became vital to establish a railroad repair shop for engines and cars. Columbia also became a transfer station, where freight was brought by rail, unloaded, and placed into other cars for transportation to its final destination. Columbia became a manufacturing town, because the manufactured item could be placed on a car and immediately shipped to a final destination, avoiding delays at a transfer station.

The bridge provided transportation from the east to points west, which included York, Baltimore, Washington D.C., and Pittsburgh. In a testament to the skill of the early Pennsylvania bridge builders, the construction of the Columbia-Wrightsville Bridge was such that it could handle the weight of railroad cars. Although it was originally built to handle nothing heavier than wagons, it could stand the massive weight – and violent vibrations – of railroad cars.

While it is not known exactly when rails were added and the first railroad cars crossed the bridge, it was most likely after 1846. In that year, the Columbia Bank and Bridge Company sent representatives to the Wrightsville Borough Council to object to its granting of the permission to the railroad to lay tracks so close to the opening of the bridge. The canal company joined in the objection. They reasoned that a spark from the locomotive caused a serious fire hazard to the bridge. When rail cars eventually were pulled across the bridge, teams of mules or horses provided the power. Locomotives were not used, all in an attempt to prevent fire to the seasoned wood of the bridge structure. There was the present danger of a spark from a locomotive smoke stack. For that reason, locomotives were not permitted to cross the bridge. When the passenger train from York arrived in Wrightsville, the "through" car for Columbia was detached, and pulled across the bridge by a team of horses or mules. This was a common operation in the early days of railroading. Still in 1859, the Pennsylvania Railroad was pulling some of its passenger cars through the streets of Philadelphia with animal power. So the practice of pulling cars over the bridge by animal power was common in 1863.

The Baltimore and Susquehanna Railroad owned the road from Baltimore to York, and used the rails on the bridge. Another was the Gettysburg and Harrisburg Railroad. The state of Pennsylvania owned the line from Philadelphia to Columbia, and the Harrisburg, Portsmount, Mount Joy and Lancaster Railroad Company owned the line from Dillersville to Harrisburg. Their cars also crossed over the bridge. The bridge was a connection for the railroads that ran on both sides of the Susquehanna. A pair of tracks had been installed on the bridge to move the cars from the shores of the river.

It was on those tracks that a trainload of Confederate prisoners had passed. In route to a Federal prison camp in New Jersey, the train was delayed for several hours in Columbia. The women of the town took food and clean clothing to the train to help relieve the suffering of the Southerners[33]. From the west, the bridge that crossed the Susquehanna from Wrightsville to Columbia was as busy as ever. There was, at first, just a noticeable increase in the eastbound traffic. At first, there were just a few residents from Franklin or Adams County, traveling with all of their worldly possessions. Alarmed by the constant news that a large Confederate force was moving north through the Valley of Virginia, those residents began an exodus that included passage of the Columbia-Wrightsville Bridge. Estimated in the thousands, the people arrived on foot, riding on horse back or on mules. Some were in carriages, others in wagons.

All wanted one thing: passage on the bridge eastward. Men, women, and children, in their vehicles of every possible description, pushed east. Some brought along their horses, cattle, sheep, or hogs. They crowded the covered bridge that replaced the earlier bridge that had replaced the ferry that John Wright, then his children, operated across the river. The bridge's toll collectors had a field day.

On the land that once hunted and controlled by the native Susquehannocks a mere 150 years earlier, the great structure connected two growing sections of Pennsylvania, providing a vital transportation artery. It was here that supplies and goods,

---

[33] Columbia Civil War Centennial. A copy is available at the Columbia Historic Society, Columbia, PA. Page 13.

people and animals, moved quickly and safely across the wide Susquehanna River.

Now those fleeing the Confederates relied on the bridge to provide for their mass departure. Some sought shelter on the farmsteads of relatives. Others were just fleeing, aimlessly, with no real plan as to where they might find a temporary place to stay or any real security. Yet in a strange way, their exodus east to Lancaster County made it even a better target for General Early.

It made the county a richer prize. The more animals – particularly the horses and cattle, the more supplies, the more the Confederates would want to invade and capture the country. The more they congregated into Lancaster, the more likely it was to attract the Confederate army.

A marker that commemorates the Conestoga Indian Town. It is about 6 miles southeast of Columbia.

Chapter 3
In Defense of Lancaster County

In Lancaster County, a sense of urgency was finally overcoming an earlier public attitude of insouciance. While the citizenry of York, Adams, and Franklin Counties seemed apathetic to the pending arrival of the Confederate army, the residents of Lancaster County took a more aggressive and defensive role. Located on the eastern shore of the Susquehanna, and having the defensive position across the river did not stop the organization of local militia groups.

Although the Susquehanna is about a mile wide between Columbia and Wrightsville, there are other places where the river is not near as wide. At points to the north and south of Columbia, the river narrows to a much shorter distance. The citizens of Lancaster County intended to defend their homeland against the Confederates. Perhaps surprisingly, the local farmers and residents, a majority from German, Quaker, Mennonite, and Amish descent, who would most likely seem pacifists, took up arms to defend their properties and families.

On June 15th, General Couch issued a special order authorizing and outlining separate areas bordering the Susquehanna River. He specified specific defense areas, describing their extent and allocating a commander for each defined area. General Couch's order defined these areas as:

- From the Maryland line at Conowingo north to York Furnace—Major Thaddeus Stevens Jr., 122 Pennsylvania Volunteers.

- From York Furnace[34] to the line of Columbia Borough—Major R. W. Shenk, 135 Pennsylvania Volunteers, Headquarters at Safe Harbor.

- Columbia Borough to Marietta—Captain Haldeman, Headquarters, Columbia.

Major General Couch issued another special order that same day. He said, in Special order #3, that "Captain C. C. Haldeman[35] is hereby authorized to raise troops and assume command of same for the defense of Columbia, Pennsylvania, the Bridge, dams, and fords in the Susquehanna River and vicinity."

Another brief order stated, "Sir: It is of vital importance that the fords and passenger bridges over the Susquehanna should be protected. You will therefore make preparations, as soon as possible to effectively guard them."

In various communities throughout Lancaster County, many different patriotic groups organized quasi-military units which had been drilled and trained for some time, and possessed firearms. They had drilled and become fairly competent in their use. Some of these groups of local men had become absorbed into the Pennsylvania militia, and others were already incorporated through regular enlistment in the Federal Army. Those that were left in the county that had at least the fundamentals of drill and military instruction were valuable additions in the assembling and organizing of the somewhat haphazardly formed groups who presented themselves at the various rendezvous. In Lancaster County, there were various points for the rendezvous:

Citizens of Conestoga and Lancaster Township at Shenks Ferry.

Citizens of Manor and Millersville at Safe Harbor.

---

[34] Prior to 1863, there was a bridge at York Furnace that spanned the Susquehanna River. This location is south of the Columbia-Wrightsville Bridge. It is at a place where the Susquehanna is narrow. York Furnace is in York County. The bridge crossed to Lancaster County near or just south of Pequea into Lancaster County. It has been destroyed years before, and never rebuilt. There was now a river ford not far away, and it was defended on the Lancaster County side by a local group of loosely organized militia, near present-day Shenk's Ferry.

[35] Captain of Company I, 23rd P.V.I.

Citizens of Columbia Borough, East and West Hempfield, Manheim Township, Manheim Borough, Warwick, Elizabeth and Rapho Townships at Columbia.

Citizens of Marietta, East and West Donegal, and Conoy, at Marietta, Etc.

From the other fifteen southeastern townships at Peach Bottom Ferry.

Martic, Pequea, East and West Lampeter Townships at McCalls Ferry.

General Couch had recognized the serious magnitude of the threat to Pennsylvania. He requisitioned equipment, rifles, and other necessaries for ten thousand men, and two million rounds of ammunition from Philadelphia. General Couch advised Secretary of War Stanton that his men available for the defense were utterly raw, and that there were only a small percentage of veterans. His artillery and cavalry were green, having never seen any action.

Even though he was an experienced and able General, his small quantity of personnel lacked in all areas. He had to make the best of a deficient in numbers and training, and a serious lack of artillery, which was essential to the success in combat of any major type. The military situation as General Couch saw it did not allow for any offensive action. At best, he might be able to mount some type of line along the Susquehanna with the green troops he had had available.

The experienced General Couch knew that at any instant the Confederates could determine the weaknesses of his defense, and quickly swing right, cross South Mountain, roll through Gettysburg and York, cross the Susquehanna, and move to Harrisburg and Philadelphia. With a rapid advance of Southern cavalry and artillery, the Confederates could capture the state capital and seize Philadelphia. The Southerners might continue marching through the Cumberland Valley, under the cover of mountain ranges, or make that right turn.

The Monday, June 15th edition of the *Lancaster Daily Express* reported that in Harrisburg all business was at a standstill, the stores were closed, and the entire population was engaged in preparations for defense or flight from the capital city.

On the same day, June 15, work began on a masonry breastwork. Located near a dam that crossed the Susquehanna, the workers of the Columbia Rolling Mill provided the labor to build the well-constructed defensive position. It required 10 days of work, but was reported to be of extremely sturdy construction. It made a perfect place to position a battery of artillery. This fort-like position was located near the southern end of Columbia Borough, about 100 yard north of the boundary line. The heavy masonry structure was located near the old flint-grinding mill.

The local newspaper took notice of the structure. It reported, "Captain W. G. Case has constructed a very formidable defense which commands the breast of the dam. This consists of a strong fort, the parapet section of which is solid masonry, containing two embrasures mounted with heavy guns. The fort is supported by other fortifications in the rear and a long section of rifle pits on the right. They are works of great strength and enfilade the entire breast of the dam."

The local population displayed enormous zest upon the completion of this impressive fortification for the town's defenses. On Saturday, June 21, there was an official flag raising ceremony. The flag was flown from the top of an enormous walnut tree near the fort.

The innovative fortification was given the name of Fort Case. The flag was raised at six o'clock that evening. About one thousand citizens of Columbia attended. There was a salute to the United States flag, several orations by local leaders, and then the firing of a nine-gun salute.

The town served a feast to those local laborers that had worked on the fortification, and to the citizens and soldiers. The food consisted of a roast ox barbecue. Captain W. G. Case and H. R. Knotwell provided the ox. Many other refreshments and food were placed on extensive tables.

It was not the first time such community celebrations were held on Columbia. On July 4, 1861, Columbia residents celebrated Independence Day with an intense patriotic fever. Several local regiments paraded through the borough's streets. There was a group of citizens singing patriotic songs in a grove near the Shawnee Run, and the Vigilant Fire Company topped off the evening by hanging Confederate President Jefferson Davis in effigy[36].

---

[36] Columbia Civil War Centennial. A copy is available at the Columbia Historic Society, Columbia, PA. Page 12.

Since the start of the War Between the States, Columbia had been contributing to the Union effort. Various local military groups had formed. The Ellsworth Rifles, the Cookman Rangers, and Birney's Zouaves were recruited from the town of 5,500. Columbia was Lancaster County's second largest community, second only to the City of Lancaster.

Company F of the Second Pennsylvania Regiment were locally known at the Shawnee Rifles. They were disappointed when they did not see any action during the Battle of Manassas. But when they returned home on July 27, 1861, the town heralded their arrival as heroes. After marching through the borough, the soldiers were served a great feast, buffet style, in the town's market house. There was a huge array of meats, pies, cakes, and the pleasing edibles of the area heaped upon long table in bountiful supply," the local press reported.

The ladies of Columbia formed the Soldiers Aid Society and set up headquarters in Jonas Myers' storeroom on Locust Street, located near the Franklin House. The reality and harshness of war hit home on December 14, 1861, when the town lost its first local son. Issac Goodwin's son John, a member of the 23rd Regiment of Pennsylvania Volunteers, died at a hospital near Washington.

By Monday night, June 15, 1863 an impromptu force of local militia formed together in Columbia for duty, with 200 Harpers Ferry Muskets and ammunition provided by a local committee. Called together by Captain Haldeman, they were assigned to patrol and outpost duty on the Columbia-Wrightsville Bridge and the York Pike.

The next day, two companies of infantry organized under the command of Captain John Peart and Noah Keesey, as well as a considerable number of unorganized mounted men, reported for scouting and outpost duty. On Tuesday evening, the Reading and Columbia Railroad chugged into town, carrying a company of men armed with their own rifles from Lititz. They were under the command of Captain Seable. They marched from the train depot to the Town Hall, where their arms were exchanged for State arms that had been provided from Harrisburg. This force was dispatched to the York County side of the river, under command of

Captain G. H. Erisman. They established outposts six miles from the river, and scouts were dispatched to York during the night.

On that same day, Captain Haldeman issued an order that "Each citizen will provide his own arms and ammunition until a supply of arms reaches this department, also rations for three days, also entrenching tools, either an axe, shovel or pick."

On June 17, the Lancaster newspaper reported that two companies arrived from Lancaster. Under the command of Captain Kelly and Captain Nevin, there was no transportation available for the company. They marched up the turnpike from Lancaster (now Route 462). As the companies were marching toward Columbia, John Sheaf, the Chief Engineer of the Reading and Columbia Rail Road, staked out the area for the laborers to dig earthworks near Wrightsville. The laborers worked all night in the trenches. The working party consisted of "over 100 Negro men from Tow Hill in Columbia.[37]

Students at Millersville's Normal School, located just a few miles southwest of the city of Lancaster, formed a makeshift militia. The sense of urgency began to bubble about a week before General Early led his Army into Pennsylvania.

Professor James Pyle Wickersham, then the principal of Millersville Normal School, organized a militia company using the school's students. Wickersham's actions were in response to the Governor's call for volunteers. Another company from Lancaster formed. Captain William Augustus Atlee's company included mostly students from nearby Franklin and Marshall College in Lancaster.

Confederate General Stonewall Jackson had directed Jedediah Hotchkiss to prepare maps of the northern states. His maps clearly identified the Susquehanna River, the roads, the canals, and the railroads all converged at this one point. From a military perspective, it was the key to control the entire area of south central Pennsylvania. It did not go unnoticed by the Southerners.

---

[37] This area was chiefly north of Fifth Street and west of Union Street in Columbia. Its name originated in the early days of the settlement when flax for weaving was grown in this area. The name "tow" refers to the flax.

The bridge that spanned the Susquehanna was exactly what Confederate General Jubal Early needed for his army to cross the river. Early and his Southerners were now on the pike that would lead them directly to it.

Both the Confederates and the Federals knew the importance of the bridge that stretched across the Susquehanna. It was a clear military objective.

On Wednesday, June 17, 1863, around noon, Wickersham's student company marched from Millersville, and headed west toward the Susquehanna River. Late that day, they had arrived in Columbia. They camped in a meadow near the Borough. They were hungry, footsore, and exhausted. The townspeople provided food to the young men of their county's militia.

Armed with the heavy muskets they had been given before leaving Millersville, the young men practiced firing their weapons the next day. They were better able to handle the weapons than their civilian instructors. Known as the Normal Guards militia company, they remained in Columbia for one week.

Supplee and Bros., a local manufacturer of rifled canon, placed one at the entrance of the bridge on June 17. The following day, General William B. Franklin, accompanied by Major Haller, 7th U.S. Infantry, now detailed as an aid on General Couch's staff at his headquarters in Harrisburg and in command at York, inspected the trenches and defenses near Wrightsville. Both military men agreed that the freshly built defenses were excellent.

Because of the shortage of volunteers, Columbia's Town Council offered a bounty of $20 for volunteers from Columbia who mustered into military service for six months or for the duration of the emergency. The Lancaster County Commissioners also offered another $20 to any enlistee.

Additional companies arrived from Lancaster County. A company consisting of men from Enterprise, Churchtown, and New Holland, under the command of Captain Redsecker and Captain Jacobs, marched into Columbia. A battery of artillery supplemented these troops under the command of Captain E. K. Young of Lancaster.

By June 20, about 600 men in total were in Wrightsville or along the York turnpike, and at the defenses erected to the west of the town. There were nine companies of infantry and one section of artillery commanded by Captain E. K. Young. The infantry commanders were Captains Seaber, Nevin, Peart, Keesey, Wickersham, Rodgers, Atlee, Ricksecker, and Cox. Lieutenant Black assumed the command of Captain Nevin's company.

Things remained confused over the next several days. Companies organized in nearby towns arrived in Columbia, but remained uncertain as to the extent of their duties. There seems to have been little effective coordination of the defense forces that was established during the first days when the alarms increased with the reports of the advancing Confederates.

It was during this period that the wounded and sick Federal soldiers housed in York were being transported to Columbia. Those that were well enough to travel were taken to the Washington Institute, and to the building at Second and Locust Streets, which was also used as a recruiting station. The town's ladies assisted in the care of the wounded at the two impromptu hospitals.

Some of the town's defenders also were excused long enough to attend a worship service on Sunday, June 21.

"Several of us attended Church today and listened to a good discourse by Rev. Mr. Smith of the Presbyterian Church here. Music has been abundant. There are glee clubs in several of the companies, one in Wickersham's company and one in Hager's. Every evening national airs and popular songs are heard through the town. We drill twice a day, and older soldiers have man jokes at the expense of the green horns," one soldier wrote.

Defenders stationed in Wrightsville and Columbia who became sick were taken to York. A Federal Hospital had been established. York's women offered aid at the two hospital buildings. The various company commands at Wrightsville and Columbia seemed to be on their own, operating in an uncoordinated matter. That was about to change.

"On Thursday, we left camp in the meadow which was the property of a Mennonite family who were "Conscientious" in everything except charging us full price for everything we got, except for some cream which was "confiscated" by some of our men,"[38] one soldier wrote about his service in defense of Wrightsville.

One section of the local population that rose to defend Pennsylvania was the local African-American community. It was at Columbia where the term "underground railroad" originated. Slave hunters from the south search for runaways along the Susquehanna. When a slave reached Columbia, they seemingly disappeared into thin air, never to be seen again. Accordingly, one hunter remarked that there "must be an underground railroad here."

One local black that established the local community was Stephen Smith. Described in a newspaper as a "prosperous, bright, and industrious Negro[39]," Smith had purchased his freedom from hard work. He toiled at General Thomas Broude's lumber yard. By age 19, he was given management of the business. Smith "attended public sales, buy lumber, of her was an expert judge, and other goods. He soon accumulated a small fortune."

Smith's success "became obnoxious to the white residents and they decided to force him to relinquish the business and sought to drive him from the town." Smith's office was on North Front Street, near the sight of the Railroad's Roundhouse. "The crowd broke into his office and completely ransacked the place."

Smith had ignored warning of white to stay away. Around August 15, 1834, a mob raided the town drove all the colored residents from their houses and destroyed their household goods, intending by this action to prevent a resettlement in the town. The Negroes fled to the hills north of though and lived in the woods.

Despite the early hardships, free Blacks reestablished their residences in Columbia. They found work at the local foundries and the railroads. They did the backbreaking hard labor that needed to be done to build the community. And now, they were ready to defend their home soil.

---

[38] Columbia Civil War Centennial, published in 1963, Page 30. A copy is in the Columbia Public Library, Columbia Pa.

[39] Sunday News, January 9, 1927. Excerpted from an article written by A. Lincoln Campbell.

The local militia, neither trained or battle-tested, remained enthusiastic. There was a great deal of singing, picnicking, and drilling.

Relatives came to visit "their boys" while they were in camp. One twelve-year old boy was asked if his older brother might actually be killed.

"Yes, but we know he will die gloriously!"[40]

General Couch had issued Special Order No. 14., placing Colonel Jacob G. Frick in charge of the defensive operations at Columbia.

SPECIAL ORDERS, HDQRS. DEPT. OF THE SUSQUE-HANNA,
No. 14.   Harrisburg, June 24, 1863.

VII. Col. J. G. Frick, Twenty-seventh Regiment Pennsylvania Volunteers, will proceed to Columbia, Pa., and take charge of all bridges and fords on the line of the Susquehanna, in Lancaster County, and make such dispositions as will effectually secure those crossings.

The commanding general calls upon the loyal citizens of Lancaster County to render Colonel Frick all the assistance that he may desire to accomplish this purpose.

Colonel Frick being in the United States service, his assignment relieves Col. E. Franklin and Major [Charles C.] Haldeman, who have heretofore been in charge. Those officers will turn over to Colonel Frick any instructions received from these headquarters.

By command of Maj. Gen. D. N. Couch:
ROBERT LE ROY,
Captain, and Assistant Adjutant-General.

With the issuance of the order, General Couch was about to drastically change the situation in Columbia. Now there would be replacements at Columbia for the citizen militia. The replacements were the 27th Pennsylvania Volunteer Militia. It was just

---

[40] Nye, Wilbur S. *Here Come the Rebels!* Louisiana State University Press, Baton Rouge, LA, 1963. 293-284.

organized in Harrisburg on June 22, 1863, and was under the command of Colonel Frick.

Colonel Jacob G. Frick was an experienced military officer. Born January 23, 1838, in Northumberland, Pennsylvania, he entered into Federal service from Pottsville, and was in charge of the 129th Pennsylvania Infantry. Colonel Frick fought at Fredericksburg, Virginia, on December 13, 1862, and later at Chancellorsville, Virginia, on May 3, 1863. At Fredericksburg, he seized the colors and led the command through a terrible fire of cannon and musketry. It was at the Battle of Chancellorsville where he engaged in a hand-to-hand fight and recaptured the colors of his regiment. By the time he was stationed at Columbia, Colonel Frick had seen his share of combat, and was battle-hardened in his own right.

When he arrived in the river town, Colonel Frick instantly took control of the bridge. His regiment went into camp in Lockhard's Hollow, and remained encamped there throughout its time in Columbia[41].

"I left Harrisburg on the morning of the 24th ultimo, and arrived here on the afternoon of the same day, and immediately sent four companies, in command of Lieutenant-Colonel Green, over the river," Colonel Frick wrote July 1, 1863, in his report.

The next day, he sent four more companies to Lieutenant-Colonel Green. He also gave instructions to take up a position near the York turnpike, about a half mile from Wrightsville.

One of the companies Colonel Frick sent from Columbia across the bridge consisted of free Blacks[42].

On Thursday, June 25, the civilian defenders were relieved when the 27th Regiment, Pennsylvania Volunteer Militia arrived from Harrisburg. On June 26, the Normal Guards militia returned to Lancaster, and stacked their arms – those old, heavy muskets -- in the Center Square.

With the arrival of Colonel Frick, the chaotic atmosphere and uncertainty from the lack of coordination each local group of volunteers vanished. Colonel Frick stationed quartered two companies in the Bridge Company's warehouse, located on the Columbia

---

[41] Columbia Spy, January 16, 1886.

[42] This group of men were never formally mustered into service.

side of the bridge. From there, they performed guard duty on the bridge. Eight companies of men had been positioned in Wrightsville, on the Joseph Detweiler farm[43].

A number of field artillery pieces had arrived by railroad in Columbia. Sitting on flat cars, the guns were useless: there was no ammo or personnel. Without gunners or shells, the field pieces sat in the railroad yard, demonstrating the confusion and inefficiency that was abound during those troublesome days.

Despite the pandemonium, the military had taken control of the Columbia-Wrightsville Bridge. It was a period of extreme activity. Troops crossed and re-crossed the bridge. The defenders were kept busy at the fortifications, making them stronger. Scouts worked the countryside on horseback, galloping back to Colonel Frick with whatever intelligence they could garner. News of the Confederates in Gettysburg, and now heading toward York, reached Colonel Frick. Reports of spies and unknown strangers in and around Wrightsville fed the frenzy.

Union General Darius Couch, the Commander of the Department of the Susquehanna.

---

[43] Close to Fourth and Orange Streets, in modern day Wrightsville.

As news of the advancing Confederates reached Columbia and Wrightsville, the military discipline allowed for an orderly assembly of the defenses. Inadequate supplies, munitions, weapons, and personnel hindered a satisfactory defense of this key entry point in Pennsylvania. The lack of artillery was a serious concern. Without support for heavy gun support, the planned defense was insufficient. Yet, under the command of Colonel Frick, the defenders continued fortifying their positions. Their entrenchments were well positioned. Their line was a considerable distance from the right and left of the York pike.

By June 26, Governor Curtin was desperate. The Confederates were within 25 miles of Harrisburg. Confederate General J.E.B. Stuart was freely roaming through parts of Adams and York counties, unopposed. Governor Curtin begged for 60,000 men. Those that did enlist into the militia were woefully inadequate. They lacked training, discipline, and experience. They were raw and untrained, and not accustomed to military discipline. They were no match for General Lee's experienced Confederate forces.

For the past two years, the citizens of the Commonwealth had heard constant calls that "the rebels are coming!" Perhaps the state's residents had become accustomed to the many false reports of Confederates raids. Southern spies were supposed to be everywhere. Maybe that is why the citizens responded so poorly to the cries of officials to join the military to defend the state's soil.

Loyal citizens of the Commonwealth passed messages via the railroad offices about the movements of the Confederates. Those messages traveled to Harrisburg, and there, at the railroad offices, were dispatched to the military office. There General Couch and his staff deciphered the messages, determining what was rumor and what was likely to be true.

Everyone at the military headquarters in Harrisburg agreed on one thing: the Confederates were likely to be at the Susquehanna by June 28. They would be either on the western shore of the Susquehanna, or have crossed it, and standing in Lancaster County.

"It was Thursday, I well remember, June 25, when everybody around here began to get pretty frightened about what might happen to us," John Q. Denny, who operated the Henry Clay Furnace, located along the Susquehanna between Chickies Rock and Columbia. "I ran the furnace. I knew it would go hard with is if the Rebels crossed the river and got hold of a place like there, where we made pig iron for cannon casting later. They surely would destroy it, and I didn't know what might happen to my family."

J. Q. Denny decided was one of the Columbia residents that decided it was best for his family to leave town while the threat of the approaching Confederates loomed.

"I decided that I would get my wife and little family away at once, to a farm where my sister Joanna lived with her husband close to the border of Chester County, about thirty miles away."

He carefully planned their escape from the Susquehanna river town.

"One of the furnace employees, an assistant foreman, a man by the name of John Williams, and I hooked up a pair of horses to an ore wagon and filled it with straw, so it made a soft bed for the children and kept the ride over the rough roads from being so hard on them and their mother."

Ore wagons had no springs, and the roads were rough and stony. About three o'clock, they left for the distant farm.

"I did not like the idea of an all night ride in a rough ore wagon," Mrs. Denny recalled. "But John knew what was best for us, and didn't know what might happen in the next few days. The children thought it was fun and played in the straw, but I didn't like the people all looking at us like we were Gypsies, or Indians. We got to Lancaster about supper time. I had some things for the children to eat, and some goat's milk. Everyone about the furnace raised goats and it was good for the children. I also had lots of bread and jam."

Mrs. Denny continued the journey through Lancaster, and down the pike to Gap. Despite darkness, she drove the wagon.

"The children went to sleep, and we rattled along down the road," she said.

"We passed through Christiana and then turned out the valley toward Smyrna, and came to Uncle Ambrose's farm in the early morning. It was just milking time, and they took us in and I fed the children who had slept through the night. I had not had any sleep so Joanna made me go to bed to get some rest."[44]

On the same day that the Normal Guard was relieved in Columbia, June 25, 1863, Confederate General Jubal Early arose in Greenwood. His men were still weary from their previous days march. There was still no indication that Federal troops were anywhere close to Early's camp. He was about 50 miles west of Colonel Frick's position.

"We were now in the enemy's country, and were getting our supplies entirely from the country people," General Early recalled years later. "These supplies were taken from mills, storehouses, and the farmers, under a regular system ordered by General Lee, and with a due regard to the wants of the inhabitants themselves, certificates being given in all cases. There was no marauding, or indiscriminate plundering, but all such acts were expressly forbidden and prohibited effectually.[45]"

The Confederates, now miles inside Pennsylvania, gathered their supplies from area farmers and shopkeepers. Paying for what they took with Confederate dollars or receipts issued for they received, the Confederates collected food.

---

[44] This account was given to J.Q. Denny, M.D., by his grandparents in 1909. Dr. Denny was then a student at the Columbia High School. A copy of this account is on file at the Columbia Historical Society, Columbia, PA.

[45] Early, Jubal A. Lieutenant General Jubal Anderson Early C. S. A. Autobiographical Sketch and Narrative of The War Between The States, with Notes by R. H. Early. J. B. Lippincott Company, Philadelphia & London, 1912. Page 255.

It was just ten days earlier that Confederate Brigadier General Albert G. Jenkins began the first part of the northern invasion. On June 15th, General Jenkins led his 1,600 cavalrymen into Pennsylvania and advanced toward Greencastle. The horse soldiers moved to Chambersburg, and stayed there for two days. The Confederate cavalry destroyed a railroad bridge at nearby Scotland. Jenkins realized he could not hold his position, and withdrew back to Greencastle on June 17. From there, Jenkins dispatched foraging parties in all directions. One of the scouting parties reached McConnellsburg. The Confederates had learned to use their cavalry to masterfully mask the movement of their main army. They were doing it again. It was during this time that skirmishes had developed between Union and Confederate forces further south, at Williamsport, Catoctin Creek, and Point of Rocks, Maryland. As General Jenkins maneuvered and raided for supplies, the Confederate army was crossing the Potomac near Williamsport, Maryland.

Word of the Confederate invasion into Pennsylvania had reached Philadelphia. It was generally thought that a full-scale movement of the Confederate army into the Keystone state was not likely. The leading editorial of the *Philadelphia Press*, of the morning of the June 17th, expressed this view:

"As we understand the situation, as it appears at midnight, there is less ground for alarm than prevailed during the day. The rebels have occupied Chambersburg, but beyond that point, no force is known to be advancing. The wires were working through to Shippensburg and Carlisle at midnight, although the rumor on the street was, that those towns had been abandoned to the enemy. This suggests to us that the rebels have too great a dread of Hooker, to divide themselves in his front, and that, while they might rejoice in the opportunity of occupying and holding Pennsylvania, they would not dare to do so, with a powerful army on their line of communications."

In the June 18, 1863 edition of the *Lancaster Express*, the paper reported, "Captain D. Bair, Jr. left Lancaster at 4:30 P.M. yesterday, (June 16) and reached Peach Bottom46 at 10:00 A.M., June 17, with the Siegel Guards. After marching to Willow Street, he reported as follows. 'Several farmers with their teams and wagons conveyed us to Buck[47], where we bivouacked for the night. Arrived Peach Bottom in the morning. Susquehanna is high at this place and it is doubted if a crossing would be attempted here." Dispatch from Peach Bottom dated June 17, 1863."

Commerce continued in Columbia. George Tillie's Grocery and Win Depot at Fifth and Union Streets advertised in the *Columbia Spy*, the town's weekly, that "Our wines are pure and unadulterated. The are suited alike to the sick and the well, the weak and the strong. Another grocery store, located at Front and Union Streets, also advertised for customers. Henry Suydam's Grocery was the place to get "the best in refined sugar, prime Rio coffee, dried fruits, and English and American pickles."

Attorneys H. M. North and H. B. Essick offered their legal services. Dr. A. S. Miller, a surgeon-dentist, worked in his office on Front Street, near Locust Street. Dr. Watson and Dr. Cottrell's office, practiced medicine and surgery next door to Cottrell's Hardware Store. And, in the dingy basement of Black's Hotel, with easy access to the bar upstairs, an agent for the Insurance Company of North America was ready to underwrite a policy for anyone needing insurance.

Samuel H. Lockard, the manager of the American House, located on Front Street, between Locust and Walnut Streets, had announced that "The bar is furnished with the choicest of liquors and the restaurant in the basement has the best in oysters, good cooking, and obligating service."

A competing bar, George Erisman's Continental Saloon, at Front and Locust, advertised, "The Continental is still kept up to the old style, and the customer will find at the bar the freshest and best Lager constantly on tap."

---

[46] A small community located along the Susquehanna River, just north of the Mason-Dixon Line in Lancaster County.

[47] A crossroads village in southern Lancaster County, about 10 miles north of Maryland.

B.F. Gray and Albert William, who owned and operated the Golden Morter Drug Store, were Columbia's leading pharmacists. More than just pills were available at the Golden Morter. One advertisement offered, "A large supply of fine brandy, old rye whiskey, and old Port wine, which we offer for sale for medicinal purposes.

This was commerce in Columbia during the American Civil War.

A few days later, there were more skirmishes between the Blue and Gray troops at Frederick and Middletown, Maryland. The skirmishes were helping the Confederates pinpoint the Federal troop movements.

On June 22nd, near present day Blue Ridge Summit, in a mountain pass called Monterey, Confederate General Jenkins ran into an armed civilian militia. The crusty, battle-hardened Confederates were no match to the rag-tag Pennsylvanians. After several minutes of fighting, the civilians were driven off. Later that same day, General Jenkins withdrew toward Hagerstown, and joined Confederate General Richard S. Ewell. There, Ewell pushed north into Pennsylvania.

By June 25, a full-scale invasion of Pennsylvania was well underway by the Southern army. Confederate General Richard Ewell followed the path of modern-day Route 11 and headed north to Chambersburg after a skirmish at Greencastle.

Near Greencastle, Confederate Generals Edward Johnson and Robert E. Rodes positioned their armies. They were two divisions of General Ewell's. To the west, Confederate Brigadier General John D. Imboden and his cavalry of 3,300 men positioned near Mercersburg. Following General Ambrose P. Hill was I Corps, under the command of Lieutenant General James Longstreet, who was always easily recognizable because of his long, bushy beard. Traveling with Lieutenant General Hill and the Confederate Army's III Corps was the commander of the Army of Northern Virginia, Robert E. Lee. To the east, near Hanover, at the Adams and York County border, Confederate General J.E.B. Stuart and his cavalry were to cross a few days later. The main Confederate army was flanked by cavalry on both sides: Imboden to the west, and Stuart to the east. And Lee's Bad Boy, General Early, was position in Greenwood.

Chambersburg was a strategic location and a key part of General Lee's plan in the invasion of Pennsylvania. It was from here that Confederate General Ewell dispatched his three divisions to continue to invasion. Chambersburg was at the heart of Pennsylvania's rich Cumberland Valley. Fifteen miles north of the Maryland border, the Confederates were sheltered from the Union Army by South Mountain to the east. The Southerners only needed to guard and block several passes through the South Mountain. This allowed the Army of Northern Virginia to move north and east. It was a perfect place for an invading force to move, by using the natural terrain to cover its movements.

Confederate General Jubal Early left his camp and men, and traveled west to Chambersburg. There he met with his commander, fellow Confederate General Richard Ewell. Generals Rodes' and Johnson's divisions had both concentrated in the area of Chambersburg.

General Ewell instructed Rodes to continue northeast, toward Harrisburg, via Shippensburg and Carlisle. General Johnson would follow. Ewell would travel with this column toward Harrisburg. General Early was directed to head east.

"In accordance with instructions received from General Lee, General Ewell ordered me to move with my command across the South Mountain, and through Gettysburg to York, for the purpose of cutting the Northern Central Railroad (running from Baltimore to Harrisburg), and destroying the bridge across the Susquehanna at Wrightsville and Columbia on the branch railroad from York to Philadelphia," Early said.

After the Columbia-Wrightsville Bridge was burnt, General Early was then to rejoin General Ewell at Carlisle, to plan for the next move against Harrisburg. Already, the Confederates had torn up the Baltimore & Ohio rail lines. General Early was to destroy the other links and return to the main Confederate column. It was a splendid plan.

As Early's men headed east, they were to be supported by Confederate cavalry.

"Lieutenant Colonel Elijah White's battalion of cavalry was ordered to report to me for the expedition in addition to French's regiment, and I was ordered to leave the greater portion of my trains behind to accompany the reserve ordnance and subsistence trains of the camps. I was also ordered to rejoin the other divisions at Carlisle by the way of Dillstown from York, after I had accomplished the task assigned me," Early said.

The military inexperience of the defenders at Wrightsville is clear. Many did not take their duty seriously, or realize the impending danger of the rapidly advancing Confederates.

One soldier wrote, "Saturday night, we had a good time. We went to the dam to fish. We couldn't catch any, but a man who had a fish trap gave us a bountiful supply and we were able to get up a supper on the portico of a family with were friendly to us. Captains Nevin, Wickersham, Atlee, and Lieutenant Black were guests. After dinner we cam some national airs, and the party broke up with cheers for the Union proposed by Captain Atlee."[48] It almost seemed as if it were a party, or summer festival, to some of the defenders.

In Columbia, the Family Medicine Store offered Lyon's Pure Ohio Catawba Brandy, as well as pure wines for sale. The wine was said to be suitable for either medicinal or Sacramental purposes. Mackerel of the finest quality, by the barrel or half-barrel, was being sold by B.F. Appold, down at the canal basin. Wallpaper, cheaper than whitewash, was sold at the bookstore operated by Saylor & McDonald, located on Front Street, near Locust. As commerce continued, no one considered that soon, all transactions could be under a Confederate flag flying in Columbia.

---

[48] Columbia Civil War Centennial. A copy is available at the Columbia Historic Society, Columbia, PA. Page 30.

Chapter 4
The Invasion of Gettysburg

After leaving the meeting, Early traveled east by horse. When he returned to Greenwood on that Thursday afternoon of the 25th, he directed all of his supply trains--except the ambulances, one medical wagon, one ordnance wagon, and one wagon with cooking utensils, for each regiment, and fifteen empty wagons for getting supplies-- sent to Chambersburg.

"No baggage whatever was allowed for officers, except what they could carry on their backs or horses, not excepting division headquarters," Early recalled. It was clear that General Early planned to move east quickly. His mind must have been racing that night as he put his head on his pillow.

Following that night's rest, General Early was ready to move his men. Cantankerous as ever, his spittle spewed as he shouted orders. He soon set the tone of his march east. In the morning on the 26th of June, just as he was ready to cross South Mountain, he came upon the Caledonia Iron Works.

It was a property owned by Congressman Thaddeus Stevens. He was the father of the public school system in Pennsylvania. Born in Caledonia County, Vermont, Stevens was as headstrong as General Early. Stevens' views and opinions never wavered. He was a determined abolitionist, and outspoken critic of the Southern system of slavery. As a member of Congress, he firmly supported President Lincoln.

The superintendent of Caledonia Iron Works attempted to convince General Early that Stevens only kept the unprofitable furnace and rolling mill open as a place of employment for the local working poor.

"That is not the way Yankees do business," General Early snapped. He ordered the forge burnt. Later he would write that he did so because Congressman Stevens "had been advocating the most vindictive measures of confiscation and devastation" against the Southern States.

General Early and his Southerners crossed South Mountain, heading east toward York. But first, the long gray line of Confederates had to pass through a little town that few outside of southern Pennsylvania had ever heard of before.

It was on the pike toward York. It was a small town called Gettysburg.

It was on the afternoon of June 26 that the 35th Virginia Cavalry battalion[49] skirmished with the 26th Pennsylvania Emergency Militia. They were leading General Early's column into Gettysburg. It was a Friday afternoon in the sleepy Adams County seat.

The 35th Virginia Cavalry had earned their nickname of the Comanches because of their use of blood-curdling cries as they attacked on horseback. Screaming and yelling war cries were part of their tradition. Soon the residents of Gettysburg would experience it first-hand.

The residents of Gettysburg knew the Confederates were approaching. During the night, the townspeople could see fires burning to the west, on South Mountain near Cashtown. It was becoming very clear that the Confederate army was edging ever closer to town.

The citizens were uneasy. News of the Confederate's invasion into Pennsylvania was printed in their newspapers. The June 19, 1863, edition of THE STAR AND SENTINEL, of Adams County, ran the following article:

REBEL ARMY CROSSES POTOMAC RIVER!
CONFEDERATES AS CLOSE AS FAIRFIELD!
- LATEST NEWS -

---

[49] Later that year, the 35th Virginia Cavalry would be nicknamed and known as the Comanches.

There has been much excitement here all week, owing to the presence of the Confederates in the neighboring Counties. The following we give as the latest intelligence and it can be relied upon:

On Friday there was a large force of the enemy at Hagerstown, probably 20,000 infantry, 2,000 cavalry, and artillery numbering twenty or more guns.

On Saturday night Jenkins' cavalry, say 2,000 were encamped a short distance beyond Waynesboro, and yesterday moved up the South Mountain. The woods were scoured by their skirmishers on foot, in advance on each side of the turnpike. When our informants left they had reached Monterey Springs, or the top of the mountain, firing at several bodies of persons on horseback on the route.

Near dusk a body of their cavalry entered Fairfield, in this county, and but eight miles from Gettysburg. Their number is estimated at from fifty to one hundred.

Because of people fleeing east from Chambersburg, word spread quickly about the Southerners. Local merchants learned how the Confederates were purchasing items with Confederates dollars or requisitions. They quickly moved their wares to a hidden or safe place, or shipped their merchandise east.

Adams County resident Robert Bell, in response to the need to defend Gettysburg, began raising an independent cavalry. He recruited men from the town of Gettysburg and from the outlying areas within Adams County. Bell, an Adams County farmer, was married to Abigail King. His ancestors, of Scots-Irish descent, served in the Continental Army during the Revolutionary War. Born in Menallen Township, located in the northern section of the county, Bell raised a company of local cavalry. Soon Captain Bell's men patrolled the roads west of Gettysburg, watching for approaching Confederates. On June 21st, about 40 men from the Philadelphia City Troop also rode into town, and joined Captain Bell and his patrol. This combined force, along with a small guard unit known as the Gettysburg Zouaves, was the borough's sole defense against any invading Confederate army. Each functioned independently of the other, and did not combine into a single unit.

Without any formal military training, Captain Bell's men soon located Confederates in the mountains west of Gettysburg. Some of Bell's men galloped back into town and reported the news.

A group of civilian volunteers decided to head west and attempt to hamper the Confederate advance by cutting down trees on the narrow roads. Marching out of town with axes on their shoulders, about fifty men soon encountered some startled Confederates. Already positioned on the eastern side of Southern Mountain, the Confederates fired some warning shots at the town's men that were there to chop down the trees. The men, including Gettysburg resident Joseph Broadhead, quickly skedaddled and returned to town when the Southerners fired upon him and the others. He returned home to his wife Sarah.

Captain Bell's men kept reporting sightings of Confederates. In response to their constant report of sightings, on Wednesday, June 24, the town received a telegram that the 26th Pennsylvania Volunteer Militia were in route and would arrive in Gettysburg the next afternoon by rail. That did not happen. Their train was derailed between Hanover Junction and Gettysburg when it hit a cow that was standing on the tracks. None of the soldiers was injured, but they did not arrive until Friday morning, June 26, around 10 a.m. Only some marched into town. The bulk of the force stayed behind.

When the 26th Pennsylvania Emergency Volunteers marched into Gettysburg, they paused long enough to receive a rousing welcome from the town.

"We don't feel much safer," Sarah Broadhead recorded in her diary[50].

Cheered on, they marched out Chambersburg Street toward Cashtown. Led by Captain Bell's Cavalry, they soon collided with some of General Early's battle hardened infantry.

The raw militiamen realized quickly how they were outmatched by the Confederates. They hurriedly fled the scene.

---

[50] Broadhead, Sarah *A Diary of a Lady of Gettysburg* Privately printed. A copy is located at the Adams County Historical Society, Gettysburg, PA.

"The officers were running around waiving their swords, shouting, and swearing, but no one dreamed of obeying them," one of the militiamen later wrote. Some fell in behind fences, while others fled through the fields.

General Early described the encounter later. "The regiment proved to be the 26th Pennsylvania Militia, eight or nine hundred strong. It was newly clad with the regular United States uniforms, and was well armed and equipped. It had arrived in Gettysburg the night before and moved out that morning on the Cashtown road. This was a part of Governor Curtin's contingent for the defense of the State, and seemed to belong to that class of men who regard "discretion as the better part of valor." It was well that the regiment took to its heels so quickly, or some of its members might have been hurt, and all would have been captured."

Around 2 p.m., riders from Captain Bell's Cavalry galloped back into town with word of the encounter. The 26th Pennsylvania Emergency Volunteers were scattering in retreat, heading northeast. Confederates not pursuing them were now on their way to Gettysburg. Bell's men, including those of the Philadelphia City Troop, dashed down York Road, spurring their horses to gallop faster. The people of Gettysburg were now defenseless.

Not many in town supposed the news to be true. For the past two years, there were constant reports that "the Rebels were coming!"

It was always unfounded rumor.

"No one believed this, for they had so often been reported as coming." Sarah Broadhead said[51].

But this time, the Rebels really were coming. They were just a few miles away, to the west of the little town.

The streets cleared. Merchants closed their stores. Schools dismissed early, sending the children home.[52]

Gettysburg teenager Tillie Pierce was born in 1848. Now at the age of fifteen, she had lived on Baltimore Street in the town

---

[51] Broadhead, Sarah *A Diary of a Lady of Gettysburg* Privately printed. A copy is located at the Adams County Historical Society, Gettysburg, PA.
[52] Alleman, (Pierce) Tillie, *At Gettysburg, or What a Girl Saw and Heard of the Battle* (1888) A copy is in the library at Adams County Historical Society, Gettysburg, PA.

her entire life. Her father was a butcher and the family lived above his shop, just south of the center of town. Tillie attended the Young Ladies Seminary, which was a finishing school near her home. She was attending school on Friday, June 26, 1863, when the cry "the Rebels are coming!" echoed once again through the town's normally peaceful streets.

"We were having our literary exercises on Friday afternoon, at our Seminary, when the cry reached our ears. Rushing to the door, and standing on the front portico we beheld in the direction of the Theological Seminary, a dark, dense mass, moving toward town. Our teacher, Mrs. Eyster, at once said, 'Children, run home as quickly as you can.'"

Soon Confederate cavalry appeared on Seminary Ridge, just one-half mile west from town. Citizens fled the streets. Doors on the stores and houses locked.

"I am satisfied some of the girls did not reach their homes before the Rebels were in the streets." Tillie recalled, "As for myself, I had scarcely reached the front door, when, on looking up the street, I saw some of the men on horse back. I scrambled in, slammed shut the door, and hastening to the sitting room, peeped out between the shutters."

The 35th Virginia Cavalry were the first to arrive in town. They turned onto Chambersburg Street, spurred their horses, and galloped toward the square, whooping and hollering, screaming and shooting in the air. The intimidation worked. There was no doubt why they were to be called the Comanches.

"The effect was enough to frighten us to death," Sarah Broadhead recalled.[53]

Gates Fahnestock, another Gettysburg resident, would later say that he "enjoyed it as if it were a wild west show."[54]

They were indeed wild and bloodcurdling. Everyone in town realized that the Rebels really were in Gettysburg.

"What a horrible sight! There they were, human beings! Clad almost in rags, covered with dust, riding wildly, pell-mell down

---

[53] Broadhead, Sarah *A Diary of a Lady of Gettysburg* Privately printed. A copy is located at the Adams County Historical Society, Gettysburg, PA.
[54] Fahnestock, Fates D. From a speech given before the National Arts Club of New York, February 12, 1934. A copy is on file at the Adams County Historical Society, Gettysburg, PA.

the hill toward our home! Shouting, yelling most unearthly, cursing, brandishing their revolvers, and firing right and left," Tillie Pierce said. "I was fully persuaded that the Rebels had actually come at last. What they would do with us was a fearful question to my young mind."[55]

"Here they come!" shouted Sarah King to her father. He was busy reading the local newspaper. He looked up and said, "Who?"

"The Rebs! Don't you hear the yell?"

The mounted Southerners galloped down York Street. They were spurring their horses, chasing Captain Bell. Sarah and her children stood on their porch, watching the thrilling chase.

"Bring the children in and lock the door," Sarah King's father said. He was concerned for their safety.

"No, I want them to see all they can of this," she answered.

The King children were indeed watching history in the making. Sarah used the unusual opportunity for her children to learn about the War Between the States. And they were about to witness even more history in the next week. Captain Bell managed to escape capture by the Confederates.[56]

Officers dispersed their men down the side streets. The Confederate infantry soon followed the cavalry, and marched into town, filing down Chambersburg Street.

"Soon the town was filled with infantry, and then the searching and ransacking began in earnest." Tillie Pierce said. "They wanted horses, clothing, anything, and almost everything they could conveniently carry away."

The infantry's march had been slowed because of the county's muddy roads. Spattered with mud and dirt, the sweaty men looked horrible, unkempt, and intimidating.

The Confederates began rounding up much needed horses. Young boys had been trying to lead them away from town, but were soon surrounded by the Southerners. Twelve-year-old Sam

---

[55] Alleman, (Pierce) Tillie, *At Gettysburg, or What a Girl Saw and Heard of the Battle* (1888) A copy is in the library at Adams County Historical Society, Gettysburg, PA.

[56] King, Sarah *A Mother's Story* Published in *The Compiler*, July 4, 1906.

Wade, Ginnie Wade's[57] younger brother, was one of the boys that was quickly captured by the raiders.

As they were passed the Pierce house on Baltimore Street, Tillie Pierce gestured to the raiders. Several rode over to her.

"You don't want the boy! He is not our boy, he is only living with us," Tillie Pierce said.

"No we don't want the boy, you can have him; we are only after the horses," one of the Confederates replied.[58]

The Confederates were on their way east to York, but wanted supplies from the merchants at Gettysburg. The Southerners looked dirty and ragged. General Early had sent advanced word that he was going to place a requisition for supplies upon the town. The Gettysburg residents knew that most of what the Confederates would want had already been removed from the community's stores.

General Early prepared a list of food and supplies that he wanted. The Confederate General rode up Baltimore Street and met David Kendlehart, the president of the borough council. The two met across from the courthouse, in front of Kendlehart's home. General Early presented his handwritten list of required supplies. General Early's levy included 7,000 pounds of bacon, 1,200 pounds of sugar, 1,000 pounds of salt, 60 barrels of flour, 10 barrels of whiskey, 1,000 pairs of shoes, 500 hats, or in the alternative, $5,000 in cash. It was a discount. The supplies General Early requested from the town were worth $6,000.

After receiving Early's requisition, Kendlehart hastily convened an emergency meeting of the town council in the law office of William Duncan. His office, located on the northwest corner of the town square, was used for the meeting. Duncan was one of the town's councilmen.

A consensus could not be reached at the meeting. Some advocated compliance while others sought defiance. Not being able to get a final decision from the councilmen, Kendlehart formed his own response to the Confederates requisition request. He located

---

[57] On July 3, 1863, Ginnie Wade became the only Gettysburg civilian killed during the Battle of Gettysburg.

[58] Alleman, (Pierce) Tillie, *At Gettysburg, or What a Girl Saw and Heard of the Battle* (1888) A copy is in the library at Adams County Historical Society, Gettysburg, PA.

General Early on Baltimore Street near the square. He told the general that it was impossible for the town to meet the demands, but that he was welcome to examine the merchant's stores to see what they could find[59].

General Early readily accepted the Kendlehart's compromise. The town's stores were opened for the inspection and use of the Confederates. General Early's troops went in search of what they needed or wanted. They found many of the shelves empty or bare.

"Nor were they particular about asking. Whatever suited them, they took," Tillie Pierce said. "But our merchants and bankers had too often heard of their coming, and had already shipped their wealth to places of safety."

The Southern soldiers eagerly flocked to the stores in Gettysburg. Under strict orders, they did not loot the stores or cause damage. What they took was purchased with Confederate currency, worthless and useless to the merchants of Gettysburg.

On Chambersburg Street, Charles McCurdy was standing outside Petey Winters' sweet shop. Although it had been closed, Petey was forced to open. A Confederate soldier walked out of the store with his hat filled with candy. "Seeing a expectant looking small boy gazing enviously at his store, (he) gave me a handful," Charles McCurdy said.[60]

At the Globe Inn, a Confederate lieutenant and three privates demanded to purchase three barrels of whiskey.

"I want good money," Charles Wills told the lieutenant as he wrote out an order on the Confederate Government. The privates rolled the barrels of spirits away as the lieutenant said, "In two months, our money will be better than yours as we may remain in your state an indefinite time."

---

[59] Will, John C. *Reminiscences of the Three Day Battle of Gettysburg at the Globe Hotel.* An unpublished manuscript on file at the Adams County Historical Society, Gettysburg, PA.
[60] McCurdy, Charles M. *Gettysburg: A Memoir.* Reed and Wittin Co., Pittsburgh, PA 1929 P.13. A copy is on file at the Adams County Historical Society, Gettysburg, PA.

Angry, Wills watched his whiskey be carried away. And he was also scared that the lieutenant's words might become true.[61]

After their scavenger hunt, some of the Confederates began moving out of town to their encampment. Their requisitioned supplies were obvious. One Southern soldier had a pair of spurs strapped onto his bare feet.

"Some of the men had a pile of hats on their heads," Sarah King said. "Blankets, quilts, and shawls were piled up on their horses."

The town's local newspapers reported the Confederate arrival in town. The Saturday, June 27, 1863, edition of THE STAR AND SENTINEL, The Republican Newspaper of Adams County, published the headline:

CONFEDERATES PASS THROUGH GETTYSBURG!
THE REBELS IN GETTYSBURG
courtesy of 'The Compiler'- "Our usually quiet town was kept in a high state of excitement all last week. Reports of the advance of the rebels upon us were brought in almost every day, but all proved untrue until Friday. On that day persons from Cashtown and vicinity reported having seen them in force. The 26th P. V. M. [Pennsylvania Volunteer Militia], Col. Jennings, was sent up the road, and when about three miles from town the rebel cavalry came upon them, captured some forty of the regiment. The balance got off, but at the time of writing [Saturday noon] we were not advised of their whereabouts.

At about 3 O'clock, sure enough, the rebel advance (cavalry) entered Gettysburg charging up Chambersburg Street at a rapid rate, in pursuit of a number of persons on horseback who were hurrying off down York Street. They fired a few shots, and the pursued were halted. In a few moments they had entire possession of the town, and their guards around it. They assured the citizens that they would not harm them, and fears should be quieted. The advance consisted of about one hundred and fifty men - White's cavalry.

In half an hour afterwards a brigade of infantry entered the town, Gen. Early in command. This brigade made up of Georgia troops, is

---

[61] Will, John C. *Reminiscences of the Three Day Battle of Gettysburg at the Globe Hotel.* An unpublished manuscript on file at the Adams County Historical Society, Gettysburg, PA.

variously estimated at from 2500 to 4000. We think the number was about midway between these two figures. Probably half of them quartered in town - in the Courthouse and on the pavements - the balance in the neighborhood. Their commander was a handsome man named General John Gordon who is a subordinate of General Early.

As soon as the rebels got here they inquired for the stores, desiring to purchase boots, hats, &c. As the storekeepers had previously removed nearly all their goods, there was little left for the rebels. However, they secured a number of hundred dollars' worth, generally paying for them, but in their own kind of money, which is not regarded as of much value here.

They captured horses in the town and neighborhood, but we presume the number was small, as nearly everything in the shape of horseflesh had been taken away days before. They 'prossed' a number of barrels of whiskey, sugar, &c., receipting therefor - payment no doubt indefinite.

Their deportment generally was civil. Many of them courted conversation, and were not disposed to interfere with anybody for exercising the largest liberty of speech. In capturing horses, &c., they made no distinctions, Democrats and Republicans suffering alike."

In the town's competing newspaper, the June 27, 1863, edition of *THE STAR AND SENTINEL*, offered their readers this description of the Confederate General that occupied their town:

THE REBEL GENERAL EARLY

Gen. Early of Virginia accompanied the Georgia Brigade that marched into Gettysburg yesterday, and immediately set about with threats of atonement for a purported bushwhacking of some of his scouts near Cashtown. The general spoke with the mayor and others to lay a levy on the borough with a time limit of only several hours to deliver the ransom. He appeared gruff in demeanor and demanded to know the name or names of the scalawags who had fired upon the scouts of White's Cavalry in the mountain pass above the town. It is a mystery as to who the assailants may have been, but one Georgia soldier told us that they had seen the body of one of their men lying by the road in a most deplorable condition, having been struck and left in the dust "like some dead animal."

We consider our fortunes to be good as it was a brigade of considerate Georgia soldiers that entered our town and not the dreaded Louisiana cut-throats called "Tigers" that we hear so much about.

During the Friday night they were in town, the Confederate troops moved seventeen railroad cars about a mile out of town and burned them. They also fired and destroyed the railroad bridge at Rock Creek. Track was torn up, and telegraph wires were cut. The Confederates discovered about 2,000 rations in a train car, which had been brought with the militia. They were confiscated and issued to General Gordon's brigade.

Thirty-six prisoners from the 26th Pennsylvania Emergency Volunteers had been housed at the courthouse. A Confederate regimental band had setup in the square on Friday night, and serenaded the town with Southern songs, including Dixie.

Elizabeth Masser Thorn was the temporary caretaker of the Evergreen Cemetery, a job normally performed by her husband Peter who was serving with the 138th Pennsylvania, which was at Harpers Ferry and Washington, D.C. during the Gettysburg Campaign. Thorn's parents, Catherine and John Masser age 63, and her three sons; Fred age 7, George age 5, and John age 2, were all living with her in the cemetery gatehouse. Elizabeth was also six months pregnant.

"It was on the Friday before (June 26) that I first saw the rebels. As the rebels came to Gettysburg, we were all scared and wished for them to go," she described her account of the events before the Battle of Gettysburg.

"Six of them came up the Baltimore Pike. Before they came into the Cemetery they fired off their revolvers to scare the people. They chased the people out and the men ran and jumped over fences...I was a piece away from the house...When they rode into the Cemetery I was scared, as I was afraid they had fired after my mother. I fainted from fright, but finally reached the house...They said we should not be afraid of them, they were not going to hurt us like the Yankees did their ladies."

Elizabeth Thorn continued, "They rode around the house on the pavement to the window, and asked for bread and butter and buttermilk...My mother went and got them all she had for them and just then a rebel rode up the pike and had another horse beside his. The ones who were eating said to him: "Oh, you have another one." and the one who came up the pike said: "yes, the -- -- shot at me, but he did not hit me, and I shot at him and blowed him down like nothing, and here I got his horse and he lays down the pike."

"He turned around to me (and) asked me, 'Is that a good horse over there?'"

"It was our neighbor's horse, and I said 'No, it ain't. It is a healthy enough horse, but he is very slow in his motions.' Well, it would not suit. I knew if the horse was gone the people could not do anything, so I helped them," Elizabeth said.

The Southerners that Elizabeth Thorn described killed the first Union soldier at Gettysburg. He just happened to be a local resident of Adams County. George Sandoe was killed. Just six days after enlisting in Bell's Cavalry, Private Sandoe had been posted on the Baltimore Pike near the Nathaniel Lightener home, sitting on his horse and talking with Daniel Lightener. Along with other troopers, Sandoe had not gotten the order to pull back. Some bushes and trees blocked the view of Confederate pickets from them. The Confederates ordered them to surrender. Sandoe's fellow cavalrymen jumped on their horses, leaped over a fence and escaped.

As Sandoe tried to do the same while firing his weapon, his horse stumbled and fell. While recovering, Sandoe spurred the horse, trying to escape, but was shot in the head by the Confederate pickets. He died on the Baltimore Pike, just two miles from his home.

Confederate General John B. Gordon.

Located about five miles south of Columbia along the Susquehanna River, this historic marker describes the earlier use of the area by Native Americans.

Chapter 5
East To York

Before leaving Gettysburg on Saturday morning, the men and officers captured by the Southerners the day before were paroled. General Early said that they were "sent about their business, rejoicing at this termination of their campaign."

Prior to their release, the captured men of the 26th Pennsylvania were relieved of their boots. General Early offered a speech to the captured men.

"You boys ought to be home with your mothers and not out in the fields where it is dangerous and you might get hurt."

After being paroled, the men started walking north, toward Carlisle.

At first light, General Early was ready to move toward York. He had spent the night northwest of Gettysburg, in the village of Mummasburg. His men had worked late the night before, searching the town for supplies. He said later "I did not have time to enforce my demands."

By 8 a.m. on Saturday, June 27, the Confederates began their march toward York.

"I then ordered Colonel White to proceed with his battalion early the next morning along the railroad from Gettysburg to Hanover Junction on the Northern Central road, and to burn all the bridges on the former road, also the railroad buildings at the Junction and a bridge or two south of it on the Northern Central, and then move along that road to York, burning all the bridges," General Early recalled. "Gordon was ordered to move at the same time along the macadamized road to York, and during the night I sent him a company of French's cavalry and Tanner's battery of artillery to accompany him."[62]

---

[62] Early, Page 258.

General Early's Confederates were on their way to the Susquehanna, but first, they had to seize York.

Back in Wrightsville, the defenders of the bridge remained ready for attack. They were feverishly digging trenches, and fortifying their defenses. The backbreaking work continued at a zealous pace. While they did not know exactly where the invading Confederates were in Pennsylvania now, word of the Rebel forces had spread throughout south central Pennsylvania. People heading east, trying to pass over the Columbia-Wrightsville Bridge, carried news about the advancing Rebels. Some of the information were rumors, other bits were facts.

The magnificent bridge that carried freight and people over the Susquehanna between Columbia and Wrightsville was the prize that Confederate General Early wanted to capture.

The bridge traffic was busy as people moved freight and supplies eastward away from York. Word of the advancing Confederates turned apathy into realization of a real emergency. Pennsylvania was invaded. The Confederate army was moving where they wanted, as they wanted, and was unchallenged. Even those that had refused to admit the most recent cries "the rebels are coming!" were true, could not deny it any longer.

For more than a week, bands of volunteers from Lancaster County's river villages watched for the advancing Confederates. Armed with shotguns and pistols, pitchforks and muskets, the locals patiently waited for the gray coats.

On Saturday, June 27, the day that General Early stood in the square of Gettysburg during daybreak, the merchants in York closed their stores at 2 p.m. The ordered closure allowed the citizens to form a militia to protect their city.

A crowd gathered in the center of the city. Recruiters opened their books, offering enrollment in a local company. Few were willing to sign up.

Word had arrived in York that the Confederates were occupying Gettysburg, a mere 30 miles away. Infantry, cavalry, and artillery units had seized the seat of Adams County. A telegraph warning from Major Granville Owen Haller, who was with the Philadelphia City Troop that had joined up with Adams County's Robert Bell, warned the city of its pending peril.

Major Haller was a York native. Born January 31, 1819, his father George died two years later. His mother, the widow with four children, was determined that each of her children would succeed. Haller's older brother graduated from Jefferson Medical College of the University of Pennsylvania. His mother wanted her son Granville to attend the Gettysburg Theological Seminary, but he had reservations. Local politics prevented him from receiving an appointment to West Point through the office of then Pennsylvania Senator James Buchanan. He was later invited to appear before a board of military officers, and was selected to enter the U.S. Army as a lieutenant. Haller accepted the position, and went on to active service in Florida and the west, slowly rising in the ranks. He saw action in various military campaigns, including the Mexican war and in several Indian wars.

In 1860, Major Haller was ordered to California, and later assigned to Fort Mojave, Arizona. Following service in San Diego, the army sent him east, to serve under General George McClellan. When he arrived, Major Haller learned that he had been promoted to be Major of the Seventh Infantry, on September 25, 1861. He also learned that his regiment had become prisoners of war in Texas, and were not able to fight against the enemy until exchanged.

Major Haller subsequently reported to General McClellan, who attached him to General Andrew Porter, the provost marshal. Soon afterwards, Major Haller was appointed commandant-general of general headquarters, on General McClellan's staff. The 93rd New York Volunteers were placed under his command as the general headquarters guard, and, when required, to guard the prisoners of war. Major Haller remained with General McClellan throughout the Virginia and Maryland campaigns, and then the subsequent campaigns of General Burnside and General Hooker.

Major Haller was then designated provost marshal general for Maryland. When it became clear that the Confederates were invading Pennsylvania, he was attached to General Couch's staff. General Couch dispatched Major Haller to York and Gettysburg to muster in volunteers, obtain all the information possible of the Confederate army's movements, and order the citizens to remove their horses, wagons, and farm stock to the eastern side of the Susquehanna River.

Citizens should arm themselves, Haller urged. Perhaps the county could be defended. Even though he was temporarily on sick leave, he worked to defend his native Pennsylvania.

York's town leaders called a meeting that evening to decide what to do. The recruiting continued for a militia.

Cavalry was an important part of the movement of Civil War armies. Cavalry troopers often advanced well in front of and on the flanks of the infantry. Serving as the eyes and ears of the main army, troopers would race back on their horses and report what awaits the advancing army. From western York County, as General Early started toward the city, the Cavalry was doing just that.

Two columns of Confederates advanced toward York, one on the macadamed road known today as Route 30. The other traveled on the road from East Berlin. It was the practice of the Southerners to travel in parallel columns, whenever possible. On both sides, General Early kept his cavalry moving, scouting, and reporting what was ahead.

As they marched east, the Confederates met no resistance. There were no Yankee soldiers or any local militia attempting to stop their advance. The fields were full of grain and corn. Cattle grazed in pastures. Well-kept barns provided visual proof of the prosperity of York County's farmers.

A brigade of Confederates had procured whiskey as they passed through Gettysburg. Now visibly and disabling drunk, they could not keep up with their column.

"The whole brigade got drunk," Lieutenant J. Warren Jackson wrote later. "I never saw such a set in my life."

The Louisiana soldiers, known as the Tigers, were so hung over that their officers threw them into a loaded cook wagon. It was not long before these soldiers begged to get out of the wagon and walk.

Confederate General John B. Gordon had time to enjoy the beautiful Pennsylvania farmland as he rode his coal-black stallion toward the Susquehanna. The plentiful, pleasant valley made an impression on the General's mind.

"It was delightful to look upon such a scene of universal thrift and plenty. Its broad grain-fields, clad in golden garb, were waving their welcome to the reapers and binders. Some fields were already dotted over with harvested shocks," General Gordon would recall and write forty years later. "The huge barns on the highest grounds meant to my sore-footed marchers a mount, a ride, and a rest on broad-backed horses."[63]

The next year, Gordon would cheat death when a bullet just missed his spine. Sitting erect on his mount, the ball ripped through his coat. A perfect posture saved him during the Battle of the Spotsylvania Courthouse.

Now 31 years in age, Gordon was born in Upson City, Georgia. Having entered the Confederate army as a Captain, he rose in rank to Brigadier-General in June, 1863. He was then placed in charge of a brigade of General Early's in the Army of Northern Virginia on April 11, 1863.[64]

General Gordon was a lucky man, especially the previous September. During the fighting at Bloody Lane during the Battle

---

[63] John B. Gordon, Reminiscences of The Civil War (New York: Scribner's, 1903), 140.

[64] Following the Civil War, Gordon became the Governor of Georgia and a U.S. Senator. He died in 1904, just three months after his book about his reminisces of the civil war was published.

of Antietam near Sharpsburg, Maryland, a minié ball passed through his calf. It did not stop him. Then, a second ball struck him higher in the same leg. He continued leading his men. A third ball smashed through his left arm. He led his men despite the muscles and tendons in his arm were mangled. One of his small arteries was severed by that minié-ball. Yet a forth ball hit him in his shoulder. Despite pleas that he move to the rear of the line, Gordon stayed in place, leading his men. He was finally stopped by a ball that hit him in the face. That one passed passing through his left cheek and came out his jaw. He fell to the ground, with his face in his cap. Then a colonel, he might have drowned in his own blood if there had not been a bullet hole in his cap. His wife Fanny had nursed him back to health.

Now as he rode through "the broad green meadows with luxuriant grasses," he was reminded of the Valley of Virginia. Gordon said, "On every side, as far as our alert vision could reach, all aspects and conditions conspired to make this fertile and carefully tilled region a panorama both interesting and enchanting. It was a type of the fair and fertile Valley of Virginia at its best, before it became the highway of armies..."[65]

During his ride to York, a natural Pennsylvania spring and the ingenuity of the Pennsylvania Dutch farmer impressed General Gordon. The farmer had built his dining room immediately over a spring. Having camped for the night was nearby, General Gordon accepted the farmer's invitation to have breakfast with him.

"As I entered the quaint room, one half floored with smooth limestone, and the other half covered with limpid water bubbling clear and pure from the bosom of Mother Earth, my amazement at the singular design was perhaps less pronounced than the sensation of rest which it produced," General Gordon said. "For many days we had been marching on the dusty turnpikes, under a broiling sun, and it is easier to imagine than to describe the feeling of relief and repose which came over me as we sat in that cool room, with a hot breakfast served from one side, while from the

---

[65] John B. Gordon, Reminiscences of The Civil War (New York: Scribner's, 1903), 141.

other the frugal housewife dipped cold milk and cream from immense jars standing neck-deep in water."[66]

When the column reached the small town of New Oxford, located between Gettysburg and York, the Confederate horsemen
traveled south to Hanover. Once there, they would move on to
Hanover Junction, and cut the telegraph lines and destroy the
bridges of the North Central Railway. If they were successful,
they could isolate Harrisburg from Baltimore and Washington,
DC.

These men were the Comanches, the same men that had rode
into Gettysburg with such flair the day before. Under the command of 31-year-old Elijah "Lige" White, a well-educated farmer
from Loudoun County, Virginia, the 35th Virginia Cavalry were
known for their war cries. He entered service for Virginia as a
private, but quickly advanced through the ranks. He became a
lieutenant-colonel, and his unit became known for getting the job
done.

About 250 strong, the Confederate horsemen rode cautiously
through the enemy countryside. They rode into Hanover unopposed, but were ready for a fight. They kept their weapons ready
for a confrontation.

While there were was no confrontation with Union troops,
things did become contentious with some of the town's merchants. While the shops were closed, and stock removed, the rebels wanted to search the stores.

One of the shopkeepers, at gunpoint, reluctantly opened his
Baltimore street store. The Confederates quickly ransacked it.

Before they left for Hanover Junction, the rebels cut Hanover
off from the rest of the world. The telegraph lines were cut, and
the telegraph was confiscated.

---

[66] Gordon,, 141.

As General Gordon progressed through the Pennsylvania countryside, he followed the orders of General Lee, which required the protection of private property. "Guided by these instructions and by my own impulses, I resolved to leave no ruins along the line of my march through Pennsylvania; no marks of a more enduring character than the tracks of my soldiers along its superb pikes," General Gordon said. "I cannot be mistaken in the opinion that the citizens who then lived and still live on these highways will bear me out in the assertion that we marched into that delightful region, and then marched out of it, without leaving any scars to mar its beauty or lessen its value."

There were two exceptions. One problem occurred when his men needed firewood for campfires. His men sought permission to use a few rails from an old-fashioned fence near one of the camps. Being after dark, the General agreed that they might take the top layer of rails, as the fence would still be high enough to answer the farmer's purpose.

By the next morning, the fence had nearly all disappeared. When questioned, each Confederate declared that he had taken only the top rail. Unknowingly, General Gordon had authorized the destruction of the fence. "There was no alternative except good-naturedly to admit that my men had gotten the better of me that time."

The Confederates, while on the move through Pennsylvania, used the Confederate "conscript law" in drafting Pennsylvania horses into their service. The Confederate Congress passed that law in order to call into able-bodied men into the Southern army, but General Gordon's soldiers seemed to think that it might be equally serviceable for the ingathering of able-bodied horses at the North.

"The trouble was that most of these horses had fled the country or were in hiding, and the owners of the few that were left were not submissive to Southern authority," General Gordon said years later. "One of these owners, who, I believe, had not many years before left his fatherland and was not an expert in the use of English, attempted to save his favorite animal by a verbal combat with my quartermaster. That officer, however, failing to understand him, sent him to me."

The "Pennsylvania Dutchman" was soon firing his broken English at General Gordon. He opened his argument with a simple proclamation.

"You be's got my mare," the Dutchman said.

"It is not at all improbable, my friend, that I have your mare, but the game we are now playing is what was called in my boyhood 'tit for tat,'" General Gordon said.

To no avail, the Confederate General tried to explain to the Dutchman that the country was at war, that at the South horses were being taken by the Union soldiers, and that he was trying on a small scale to balance accounts.

"I flattered myself that this statement of the situation would settle the matter; but the explanation was far more satisfactory to myself than to him. He insisted that I had not paid for his mare," General Gordon explained.

The General offered to pay him for the horse--in Confederate money. He had no U.S. dollars. The Dutchman refused.

"Finally I offered to give him a written order for the price of his mare on the President of the United States. This offer set him to thinking. He was quite disposed to accept it, but, like a dim ray of starlight through a rift in the clouds at night, there gradually dawned on him the thought that there might possibly be some question as to my authority for drawing on the President."

The suggestion of this doubt exhausted the Dutchman's patience. He had little fear in dealing with a Confederate General.

"In his righteous exasperation, like his great countryman hurling the inkstand at the devil, he pounded me with expletives in so furious a style that, although I could not interpret them into English, there was no difficulty in comprehending their meaning. The words which I did catch and understand showed that he was making a comparison of values between his mare and his "t'ree vifes."

"I 've been married, sir, t'ree times, and I vood not geef dot mare for all dose voomans," the Dutchman told General Gordon

Getting nowhere, an exasperated General Gordon gave in. Maybe it was the argument that the mare was better than any of his three wives.

"I finally yielded to his entreaties and had her delivered to him," General Gordon said.

The persistent Pennsylvania Dutchman left the General's presence, calmed down, and with his mare in hand.

General Early pushed toward York. It was about a 20-mile march that Saturday. Somewhere west of York, a *New York Herald* reporter had caught up with a well-dressed Confederate Major-General mounted on a horse.

"I have no time to attend to you just now," the general snarled at the reporter. He was not discourteous, but was, as always, sharp.

York City resident Arthur Briggs Farquhar was young and an enterprising businessman. He had arrived in York seven years earlier. Born and raised in Sandy Spring, Maryland, Farquhar, a Quaker, had attended the Hallowell School in Alexandria, Virginia. Years before, so did General Robert E. Lee.

Farquhar apprenticed in a machine shop. Four years after arriving in York, he took a bride. In 1860, Farquhar married Elizabeth Jessop, the daughter of a prominent local businessman Edward Jessop, in a Quaker wedding.

Coming to York at the age of 17, and before his marriage, he traveled to New York City. There he gained audiences with A.T. Stewart, William B. Astor, James Gordon Bennett and other men of substantial means.

Farquhar always asked them one simple question.

"How can I make a million dollars?"[67]

Now with a fledgling business to protect, A. B. Farquhar was not about to have everything lost by having York fired upon by the approaching Confederates. A.B. Farquhar had made valuable business contacts in the South while representing his company. At the beginning of the road to his first million dollars, the 24-year-old entrepreneurial Quaker was not prepared to take a wait-and-see what the Confederates would do attitude.

---

[67] James McClure, East of Gettysburg (York: York Daily Record, 2003), 44.

Some citizens of York probably dismissed the cries of "the rebels are coming!" For weeks, word had spread the gray coats were coming, yet they had not. It has been nothing but a series of false alarms. Of those that doubted the arrival of the Confederates, little did they realize that General Early's columns were marching directly toward their city. Infantry, cavalry, and artillery of the invading enemy were getting closer.

Time passed on Saturday. Those that remained in York were uneasy, as was A.B. Farquhar, and the town's fathers.

The Committee of Safety held an emergency meeting in the counting room of P.A. & S. Small's store. It was at that meeting that A.B. Farquhar advocated making a deal with the Confederates. He argued that the town could make a better deal in advance of their arrival. Farquhar told the members of the Committee of Safety that when the Confederates marched into town, they would quickly realize how little had been moved across the river.

In latter part of June, some of the citizens of the Commonwealth in Harrisburg, Pittsburgh, and other locations had prepared for the Southern invasion by digging fortifications. Many south-central Pennsylvanians clogged the country and town's roads, all in a desperate effort of driving livestock northward and taking their belongings beyond the enemy's reach. Others did little in preparation.

In spite of Governor Andrew Curtin's repeated calls for volunteers to defend the Commonwealth against the Southerners, citizens responded far less than enthusiastically. After Governor Curtin's final plea for sixty thousand recruits, only sixteen thousand Pennsylvania men had come forward to enlist. Both the New York militia that hurried to the state capital of Harrisburg as well as invading Confederates, noticed an overabundance of military-age men loitering on town streets, seemingly indifferent to the state's crisis.

York seemed to have an abundance of supplies – and military age men. As historians would remark for decades afterwards, this was not the town's finest hour. The Committee met in Smith's Hardware, at the town square. It was in the same town where the Continental Congress had convened for nine months during the American Revolution. It was within the borders of York that the new fledgling country called itself the United States of America.

The same spirit and dedication of those men that declared independence from England and fought the British army vanished within the streets of York.

York lawyer Thomas E. Cochran offered his legal opinion of Farquhar's plan. It was full of flaws. Who would go and negotiate with the Rebels? Could the town keep its bargain, and most importantly, would the Confederates honor their part of the agreement? In response to Cochran's concerns, A.B. Farquhar offered to meet the Confederates as an emissary.

York's leaders did not view the young businessman's proposal seriously. They dismissed his plan.

Farquhar refused to accept their decision. He told the member of the Committee that he would go to the Confederates and meet with them anyway.

Determined as ever, the Quaker hitched up his horse to a buggy, and traveled west out of town. Maintaining a steady pace westward on the pike toward Gettysburg, A.B. Farquhar was intent on asking the Confederates about their plans with York.

Farquhar found the Southerners about 15 miles west of York, near the small community of Abbottstown. As he approached their lines, it did not take him long to locate a former school friend, Lieutenant Redik from Georgia.

"Hello, Farquhar," Redik said, "What are you doing up here among the Yankees?"

"I came just to find out what you are doing up here among the Yankees. I have some property in York, and I don't want it burned," Farquhar told his friend.

Lieutenant Redik escorted A.B. Farquhar to meet General Gordon, whom the York Quaker had an acquaintance through mutual friends.

"What's your business?" General Gordon asked.

"General Gordon, unless you have entirely changed from the character you used to have," Farquhar said, "you are neither a horse thief nor a bank robber, and fighting is more in your line than sacking a city."

General Gordon inquired as to what Farquhar was suggesting. Farquhar proposed that the general and his men enter York quietly — without any opposition — and make reasonable requisitions. The town's leaders would see that they are honored.

Farquhar asked General Gordon to sign the notes of their meeting. Farquhar assured Gordon that his signature would give him validity with the Committee of Safety back in York. It would also ease the minds of the town's residents, including women and children who were terrified. Gordon said he was glad to spare the noncombatants from the horrors of war, unlike the actions of the Federal troops in Virginia. General Gordon signed Farquhar's notes of the conversation, stating that the Southerners would not confiscate private property or molest anyone but would expect necessary supplies.

General Gordon questioned Farquhar about the forces guarding York. Sometime during the conversation, the Confederate General produced a map of York County that proved the Confederates were well prepared.

When the meeting had ended, A. B. Farquhar had a deal – in writing -- with Confederate General Gordon. No property would be destroyed, private businesses would remain unharmed if the Confederate army gained provisions and clothes, and women in town would be respected. The slightest indignity offered to any lady by the Southerners would be punished with immediate death.

Farquhar prepared to return to York with the deal. General Gordon balked, but the persuasive Quaker prevailed. The young A.B. Farquhar gave his word of honor that he would reveal nothing. If there were any resistance, he would return to the General's lines to be hanged as a Northern spy.

Farquhar did not obtain any passwords to head home through the Confederate's line. Lieutenant Redik told him that if anyone tried to stop him, he should just give the horse rein. After the last outpost, he traveled about 100 yards down the pike, and then rebel bullets started flying past him. Farquhar raced to York and pushed his horse for all the speed it could muster.

When A.B. Farquhar returned to York, he found Major Granville O. Haller was defending the town. He had a small force, not more than 350 in size. It would have been no match for General Gordon and his battle-hardened gray coats.

York's leaders did not approve of Haller's presence, his force, or the preparations to defend the town.

"This movement was not appreciated by the Citizens, who, apprehensive that a collision might subject the town to the vengeance of the enemy," Haller later wrote, "believed it would do the inhabitants much injury."

Major Haller and A.B. Farquhar walked to Smalls' store, where the Committee of Safety contemplated what to do next. Farquhar told the members of the Committee that a large force of Confederates was en route to York. Nevertheless, he was honor-bound not to say anything more.

Haller doubted Farquhar. He did not know him. A native of York, Haller had served in the U.S. Military for the past two decades. Being gone so much of the time, Major Haller did not know the people that had recently settled in York.

Cochran, one of the town's lawyers, did what lawyers do so well: vexed. In typical attorney fashion, Cochran reasoned that if the Confederates discovered that Farquhar had lacked authorization to make the surrender agreement, the Southerners would not need to honor their part of the deal. Farquhar, as well as others, including members of the Small family, urged that members of the committee enter Confederate lines to arrange the terms, making the agreement official.

The members of the Committee of Safety decided to meet the Southerners west of town, and to ascertain the terms of Farquhar's surrender agreement. They also decided that Major Haller's defense force should withdraw to the Susquehanna. Sending Major Haller to Wrightsville, the civilians overruled the military command.

From York, Major Haller sent a message to General Darius Couch.

"Off toward Wrightsville and Columbia. The enemy approaching with the Gettysburg force, about 4,000. Will respect private property if not resisted, and borough authorities wish no resistance."

He signed the message G.O. Haller, Major Seventh Infantry, and Aide-de-Camp.

As Haller and his men prepared to ride east to defend the bridge at Wrightsville, Farquhar and the others prepared to ride west, to meet with General Gordon, and surrender the town of York.

About 350-men in strength, Major Haller's ragtag force of defenders started their 12-mile trip east to Wrightsville. Some marched, others rode the train, and some made the trek on horseback. It was an assorted, haphazardly assembled troop that consisted of detachments from the 20th Pennsylvania and 26th Pennsylvania Emergency regiments, a part of Captain Bell's Cavalry, the Philadelphia City Troop, a detachment from the 87th Pennsylvania that fled to York after the Battle of Winchester, the Patapsco Guard, and some invalid soldiers that were convalescing in York. Ill equipped, ill prepared, and small in number, those brave soldiers had stood prepared to defend York – its citizens and their property – against a large invasion advanced by the Confederates. Now, asked to leave, they assembled to head east, to take up a defensive position near the prized military target that spanned the Susquehanna.

To the sound of drumbeats, the force of defenders marched east. York was defenseless.

It remained at the mercy of General Early.

The citizens had to worry about their fate as they watched Major Haller's brigade leave the former U.S. Capital.

That evening, General Gordon stopped at a house in the small village of Farmers. As was often the procedure, a general would setup his headquarters in someone's home, while his soldiers camped in surrounding pastures and fields.

General Gordon had done just that, setting up his field headquarters in the home of Jacob S. Altland. He was about 10 miles west of York.

The local farmers were courteous and generous to General Gordon. The Southerners cooked their food in iron pots, pans, and skillets. The farmers assumed that their generosity might garner kinder treatment from the Confederates.

Following the meal, Confederate bands played music, and many of the soldiers joined in singing. Spirits ran high that night, just west of York.

The next day, the Confederate soldiers expected to see the Susquehanna. They wondered what the Yankees might have prepared for them.

The troops that had been defending York against overwhelming odds finally arrived in Wrightsville. It was about 7:30 p.m., Saturday evening. Having been asked – or directed -- to leave by the members of the Committee of Safety, this group of brave defenders finally reached the western shore of the Susquehanna.

"A scene presented itself which can hardly be exaggerated," Major Haller wrote later. "Locomotives, tenders, and cars of all descriptions lined the railroad, awaiting removal to Columbia."

The small town of Wrightsville was not prepared for what was coming at them from the west. General Gordon's troops were but one day away. They were woefully unprepared.

When Major Haller arrived in picturesque Wrightsville, he found the equivalent of a modern day traffic jam.

"The turnpike road leading the bridge was lined with large wagons, removing property of citizens across the Susquehanna," he said. "There was much time lost by teamsters having to halt and pay toll and the transportation agents not have sufficient animals for the extraordinary demand upon them."

Major Haller obtained quarters for his command. He arranged for their suppers, and then sought Dr. Barton Evans, the president of the Columbia Bridge Company. Major Haller pointed out the lengthy detention at the bridge entrance, and urged that the toll collectors stop charging for passage. Up to this point, the toll collectors had enjoyed brisk business, collecting for every person, wagon, or livestock that crossed.

Dr. Evans agreed. Immediately the Columbia-Wrightsville Bridge was opened to travel free of charge.

Workers gathered teams of horses to remove the rolling stock. The crossings became exceedingly heavy. The work went on throughout the night.

"On the Saturday before the fire there was a continual of horses, wagons, large and small teams, cattle crossing the bridge, the whole procession were fleeing from the approach of the Confederates troops," Columbia attorney Hugh M. North said.[68]

It was late that evening when Major Haller met Colonel J. G. Frick, the commanding officer of the 27th Pennsylvania Militia. The commanders of the militia had positioned their troops in a horseshoe pattern around the entrance of Wrightsville.

"I found him confident of the courage of his troops, and eager to resist anything like a raid to destroy the bridge," Major Haller said. [69]

A.B. Farquhar prepared to return to General Gordon's camp. Accompanying him was York's Chief Burgess, David Small. George Hay, a retired colonel from the 87th Pennsylvania, Latimer Small, and Thomas White, both local businessmen, completed the delegation. They headed west around 8 p.m. Saturday evening.

As they left, some of York's residents debated if the large United States flag should fly from the pole in Centre Square, or if they should take it down.

Some wanted to take it down, fearing a Confederate reprisal if they see it waving. Others argued the Rebels should see the Stars and Stripes. It was here – in York – where the country's forefathers developed and enacted the Articles of Confederation, their first attempt at governing the new nation. It was here that they fled from Philadelphia, trying to avoid capture from British troops. It was here that they stood their ground, determined in resolve to be independent from Britain and the King's rule. For nine months, York served as the nation's capital. Now the former capital of the United States of America was to be surrendered to an invading force. And the townspeople wondered what should become of the U.S. Flag, the symbol of where the town's allegiance rested.

Once again, York's Committee of Safety decided what to do. The United States stars and stripes flag would remain atop the

---

[68] From Hugh M. North's sworn deposition made August 19, 1904, before Henry B. Bruner, Notary Public.
[69] From the report of Major Granville O. Haller, Seventh U.S. Infantry, filed July 21, 1863 from York, PA. It is now in the Appendix of the War of the Rebellion: a Compilation of the Official Records of the Union and Confederate Armies, 1880-1891. Chapter XXXIX, Part III, Page 995.

city's flagpole. The Committee of Safety also resolved, "That, finding our town defenseless, we request the Chief Burgess to surrender the town peaceably …"

Following the crucial decision of the committee, the group of five of York's citizens, carrying a white flag of truce, headed west out of town. Their mission was to search for Confederate General Gordon.

Just west of Thomasville, they located General Gordon at his headquarters at the small rural village Farmers. Not much more than an intersection and crossroads on the York to Gettysburg turnpike, Farmers consisted of a cluster of several homes and some farms. The crossroads hamlet was on the rolling hills situated about seven miles west of York.

The delegation of York's representatives formally surrendered their town to the Confederates. They asked for protection for the people of the city and their property.

General Gordon told the delegation what he had told Farquhar earlier in the day. Gordon reiterated that he did not intend to pursue the Union Army's style of warfare against the borough of York. Private property of the citizens would be respected. The townspeople of York would not suffer any indignities. General Early would determine the details for provisions that he needed when he arrived in town.

General Gordon questioned the delegation about the town's defenses. He was shrewd enough to see if this group of five was being honest with him, or were nothing but subterfuge. The general already knew a lot about the defenses of York. He knew how many men guarded the town, who was in command, the troop strength at Harrisburg, and even who the key people were in town — along with their individual politics.

The intelligence the Confederate General had did not come as a huge surprise to the people of York. For the past weeks, there had been reports of mysterious strangers in town. One of them was a one-armed man dressed in a Union uniform. The puzzling visitor had demonstrated skillfulness as a stonecutter, but he refused payment. Another stranger in town was a religious book salesperson. The Bible peddler was later observed riding near General Gordon when the rebel column entered town.

With their business finished with the Confederate leader, the York officials asked to leave his encampment. General Gordon initially refused but then granted their request. The five York leaders headed east to town.

"A committee composed of the mayor and prominent citizens, met my command on the main pike before we reached the corporate limits, their object being to make a peaceable surrender and ask for protection to life and property," General Gordon later said of his meeting with York's leaders. "They returned, I think, with a feeling of assured safety."[70]

The Committee of Safety later stated that neither party talked about surrender and refused to call their deal with the Confederates a surrender. But their town was to be occupied by the Southerners. There would be no defense or opposition.

After leaving Gettysburg early in the morning of June 27, General Early and his column had an uneventful day. He traveled east, taking a route north of General Gordon, riding through Hunterstown, New Chester, Hampton, and East Berlin. Old Jube finally stopped for the night somewhere east of East Berlin, near the York and Adams County border. He stopped at the Zinn home, in Big Mount, a larger house with a porch.

Mrs. Zinn, an aged woman, met General Early at the end of the lane. In broken English, she asked the Confederate if he was "going to destroy us? Are you going to take all that we got?"

"No Madam, and to give you the best protection provideable, I will stay with you and no one shall trouble you," General Early replied. The woman admitted she was a copperhead, a Southern sympathizer.

Before sleeping for the night, General Early rode across the countryside several miles to meet with General Gordon. At his camp at the Altland residence, setup on the York Pike, General Early found General Gordon resting on a feather bed. The two Confederates discussed their plans to move against York, should

---

[70] John B. Gordon, Reminiscences of The Civil War (New York: Scribner's, 1903), 142.

it be occupied and defended by militia or Union forces. General Early had learned that General Gordon was told that the town remained undefended. He also learned of the planned surrender of the borough by the town's authorities.

"I rode over to Gordon's camp, on the York pike, which was about 4 miles distant, to arrange with him the manner of the approach upon York, if it should be defended. But all the information we could gain induced me to believe there was no force in York, and that night a deputation from the town came out to Gordon's camp, to surrender it. I directed General Gordon, in the event of there being no force in York, to march through and proceed to Columbia Bridge, and secure it at both ends, if possible," General Early said.[71].

Sometime, within the past days, General Early had decided to try to capture the bridge. Although he had orders to destroy it, clearly late on June 27, he was planning to capture it and use it. Perhaps his long hours in the saddle on his horse gave the General time to concoct the plan. Whenever he decided, it was now clearly his objective. While his commander had ordered the bridge to burned, General Early decided that he could get across the Susquehanna, take Harrisburg, then move east, and capture Philadelphia.

After conferring with General Gordon, Early returned to his camp east of East Berlin for the night. General Gordon went to sleep on the feather bed. General Early ate fresh vegetables prepared for him by Mrs. Zinn and her teenage daughter.

"Is Stonewall Jackson dead, sure enough?" Mrs. Zinn asked General Early.

"Unfortunately, madam, he is dead," General Early informed her.

At about the same time General Early was riding to meet General Gordon, Colonel Frick ordered the remaining of his

---

[71] Jubal A. Early Lieutenant General Jubal Anderson Early C. S. A. Autobiographical Sketch and Narrative of The War Between The States, with Notes by R. H. Early. J. B. Lippincott Company, Philadelphia & London, 1912. 259.

troops in Columbia to cross the bridge, and take defensive positions in Wrightsville.

"Hearing, on the afternoon of the 27th, that the enemy were in the vicinity of York, I ordered my two remaining companies to report to Lieutenant-Colonel Green, that we might be prepared to resist any sudden attempt by the enemy to get possession of the bridge at this point," Colonel Frick said.

Colonel Jacob G. Frick, Commander of the 27th Pennsylvania Volunteer Militia.

The Pennsylvania Historic Marker located in Columbia near the present-day Rt. 462 bridge.

Chapter 6
York Surrenders

Throughout the night, the work continued in Wrightsville. Everything focused around the Bridge.

The main artery was built to accommodate wagon and foot traffic. It was also used to town canal boats across the river. Rails were added, accommodating all kinds of rail cars. Teams of horses or mules routinely pulled the railroad cars across the bridge. The fear of a spark from a locomotive igniting the covered bridge was real. Its aged lumber was ready tinder.

As the traffic from the western shore moved across the bridge, Major Haller caught some needed rest. Early in the morning, he arose and "sent at once for intrenching tools." Along with Colonel Frick and Major Haldeman, he checked "the approaches and traced out the line of rifle-pits and positions for our troops."[72]

The logjam had been broken at the bridge. Now that the bridge was open without collecting tolls, refugees and their wagons had moved to the eastern shore of the Susquehanna. Using his military authority, Haller requisitioned teams of horses and mules, whose owners were keeping them safely on the Columbia side of the river. By sunrise, their all night work was apparent. The teams had repeatedly crossed the bridge, and hauled loads east. The traffic jam in Wrightsville had cleared.

The delegation of the five York residents returned to the borough at 1:30 a.m. Immediately they passed word that a deal had been reached with the Confederates. An immense Southern army would march down the town's streets later that day.

---

[72] From the report of Major Granville O. Haller, Seventh U.S. Infantry, filed July 21, 1863 from York, PA. It is now in the Appendix of the War of the Rebellion: a Compilation of the Official Records of the Union and Confederate Armies, 1880-1891. Chapter XXXIX, Part III, Page 995

There should be no resistance, they said. If there were, the rebels would surely burn the town to the ground. Nothing would remain. Instead of fighting, the citizens of York would become voluntary prisoners of war.

"We felt so relieved that all was settled," Cassandra Small wrote in a letter.

Sunrise came at 4:39 a.m. that Sunday morning[73]. General Gordon's Georgians stirred early that summer morning. They had encamped in scattered formation in the fields near Farmers. His six regiments, the 13th, 26th, 31st, 38th, 60th, and 61st Georgia were rugged and tough. The Confederates commanders formed the men into four columns. They were a force of 1,912 men.[74] W.A. Tanner's Courtney Virginia Artillery, which was equipped with four 3-inch Ordinance Rifles, supplemented them. There were also several dozen of the 274 men of the 17th Virginia Cavalry.

All remained quiet in York until around 10 a.m. Sunday morning.

Church bells in the town's steeples called the residents to worship services. Dressed in their Sunday best, the residents walked to their churches.

The ringing church bells were soon muffled as shouts passed through the town's streets.

"The rebels are coming!"

Everyone in York had heard that before.

This time, it was true.

To the west of town, a large cloud of dust was rising. It was caused by the marching and shuffling feet of the Southerners.

Without warning, suddenly a picket appeared on a street corner. Then another. The dusty, dirty Southerners were taking their assigned positions in the borough. First appearing on Market Street, then Philadelphia, George, and Duke streets, they were part of the 31st Georgia, under the command of Colonel Clement

---

[73] United States Naval Observatory. http://aa.usno.navy.mil/data/

[74] Schaefer, Thomas K. *A Matter Never to be Forgotten* York Sunday News, York, PA. 5 June – 17 July, 1988.

A. Evans, who was the provost marshal. His guards were posted to protect the advancing troops, and maintain order in the town. They were also placed in position to prevent the Southerners with parched-throats from destroying private property. They were particularly careful to guard the town's taverns.

With the sentries in position, General Gordon's brigade emerged from the dust clouds. Breaking into three columns, the main force marched down Market Street. Gordon's regiment flag flapped in the wind, as did the Confederate flag. Their band played *Dixie* and other Southern tunes.

They were grimy, dirt covered, and ragged.

"The church bells were ringing, and the streets were filled with well-dressed people," General Gordon said. "The appearance of these church-going men, women, and children, in their Sunday attire, strangely contrasted with that of my marching soldiers."

What a contrast it must have been on Market Street in York. The residents, dressed in their best for Sunday worship services, were appalled at the first appearance of the Confederates. They were, after all, the troops that had marched with General Stonewall Jackson. Surely they would be well equipped, shined, polished, and look impeccable.

Instead, the first of the Southerners that marched into town carried shovels, axes, and pickaxes. These men had the thankless but necessary job of clearing or widening a road so the following troops and equipment could advance. They were grimy, ruffled, and filthy. They carried their tools as if they were rifles. They looked like bearish cave dwellers, dressed in a mixture of well-worn gray and butternut uniforms. They smelled from their sweat and body odor. Many were shoeless or shirtless, or both. In addition, these men were detailed to dig the graves of fallen comrades or dead horses.

On seeing these grimy men, one York woman began praying.

"Oh heavenly Father, protect us. They are coming to dig our graves!"

Those Southerners, while marching forward, glanced side to side, and noticed the women adorned in their best clothes.

"Begrimed as we were from head to foot with the impalpable gray powder which rose in dense columns from the macadamized pikes and settled in sheets on men, horses, and wagons, it is no wonder that many of York's inhabitants were terror-stricken as they looked upon us," General Gordon said.

"We had been compelled on these forced marches to leave baggage-wagons behind us, and there was no possibility of a change of clothing, and no time for brushing uniforms or washing the disfiguring dust from faces, hair, or beard. All these were of the same hideous hue."

As the Confederates arrived in town, there was another spontaneous debate about the U.S. Flag flying on the town's flagpole.

"Is it possible I have lived to this day to see the flag torn down and trampled in the dirt?" York attorney John Evans pleaded to his fellow town residents.

Some agreed with him. Others wanted the flag to continue to fly proudly from the pole on the site where Congress had met 86 years earlier. Back then, they fought to bind the states together, and now came an invading force dedicated to ripping those bonds apart.

"Let them take the flag, and I will replace it," Latimer Small proclaimed.

His statement ended the debate.

At the age of 66, Brigadier General William "Extra Billy" Smith was old enough to be most of his men's father, if not their grandfather. A colorful and politically well-connected man from Virginia, Extra Billy was known throughout the North and the South. The former governor of Virginia, Extra Billy got his nickname because of the Federal contract he held to deliver mail from Washington to Georgia. He added on lots of spur routes, a fact that became known for the "extras" he was able to bill the government for services.

General Smith changed his uniform at his whim. He would sometimes where a raccoon hat. He was also seen on the field carrying an umbrella, and raising it during thunderstorms. Now he was a part of Early's division, in command of his brigade of 800 men.

Smith's brigade was at the head of the Confederate column as it entered York. The men depended on Extra Billy to cheer up the drudgery of the brigade's marches with his vibrant personality and gift for speechifying.

Smith rode into York with his hat off, bowing right and left to the amused crowds, saluting the girls with his hearty vote-getting smile. When the head of the column reached the town square, his men stopped to deliver a hearty cheer for the old Governor of Virginia.

The people of York moved forward for a better look, and the Confederate column was surrounded. It could go no further.

General Smith never met an audience he did not like, even if they were Northerners. He could not resist the opportunity for some of his silver-tongued oratory. He ordered the clearing of enough room for his men to stack arms, and launched into a rattling, humorous speech from his saddle. Forever the politician, the crowd applauded wildly for the old smiling general. Pennsylvanians and Confederates alike could not resist the pleasant and folksy words from this gifted politician.

As the silvery oratory flowed to cheers and applause, the mostly irritable General Early arrived from the rear of the column. Early was in no mood for one of Extra Billy's political speeches. He lounged intolerantly toward the center of the crowd.

Smith spewed his words as eloquently as ever. He was unaware that his spiteful commander had joined the crowd, until Early caught his blouse, jerked him around and screamed, "General Smith, what in the devil are you about, stopping the head of this column in this cursed town!?"

"Having a little fun, General," Smith replied good-naturedly, "which is good for all of us."

Unpredictably, Early cooled swiftly. The man in his clasp was, above all, the former governor of Virginia. Most likely, he would be so again.

"Halting on the main street, where the sidewalks were densely packed, I rode a few rods in advance of my troops, in order to speak to the people from my horse," General Gordon said. "As I checked him and turned my full dust-begrimed face upon a bevy of young ladies very near me, a cry of alarm came from their midst; but after a few words of assurance from me, quiet and apparent confidence were restored."

General Gordon's tone was one of assurance, despite the grimy appearance of his troops.

"I assured these ladies that the troops behind me, though ill-clad and travel-stained, were good men and brave; that beneath their rough exteriors were hearts as loyal to women as ever beat in the breasts of honorable men; that their own experience and the experience of their mothers, wives, and sisters at home had taught them how painful must be the sight of a hostile army in their town; that under the orders of the Confederate commander-in-chief both private property and non-combatants were safe; that the spirit of vengeance and of rapine had no place in the bosoms of these dust-covered but knightly men; and I closed by pledging to York the head of any soldier under my command who destroyed private property, disturbed the repose of a single home, or insulted a woman."

One of General Gordon's troops spotted the United States flag in front of the Courthouse. He pulled down the flag, and ran away with it.

A.B. Farquhar begged the Southerners not to raise their own flag.

General Gordon complied, but not without qualifying he might change his mind, and fly it anyway.

Farquhar suggested that the Confederates camp at the hospital on the commons. If they camped there, he reasoned in his own mind, the rebels would not burn the buildings that provided them shelter, and were so close to private residences. That is what he hoped.

"The grotesque aspect of my troops was accentuated here and there, too, by barefooted men mounted double upon huge horses with shaggy manes and long fetlocks. Confederate pride, to say nothing of Southern gallantry, was subjected to the sorest trial by the consternation produced among the ladies of York," General

Gordon said. "In my eagerness to relieve the citizens from all apprehension, I lost sight of the fact that this turnpike powder was no respecter of persons, but that it enveloped all alike--officers as well as privates."

General Gordon's brigade did not remain long in York. He continued east, toward Wrightsville. Soon they marched another two miles, stopping for rest at an old stone building along the York-Wrightsville Pike. From there, it was just 10 miles to Wrightsville.

As Gordon's men marched through town, some York residents noticed markings on knapsacks carried by the Southerners. It was the 87th Pennsylvania Volunteers, taken from them at Winchester. Many of the town's sons belonged to the 87th Pennsylvania, and they were still unaware if they had survived the battle that had occurred in the Virginia town. Some of Gordon's artillery pieces and wagons also bore U.S. insignias.

Some of York's residences peered through the crack of drawn parlor curtains or through the louvers of closed storm shutters.

A copperhead[75] provided General Gordon with some military intelligence about the Columbia-Wrightsville Bridge. He received it as rode through York.

"As we moved along the street after this episode, a little girl, probably twelve years of age, ran up to my horse and handed me a large bouquet of flowers, in the centre of which was a note, in delicate handwriting, purporting to give the numbers and describe the position of the Union forces of Wrightsville, toward which I was advancing," General Gordon said. "I carefully read and reread this strange note. It bore no signature, and contained no assurance of sympathy for the Southern cause, but it was so terse and explicit in its terms as to compel my confidence."

Two days earlier, it had rained in south central Pennsylvania, turning the dust on the roads into mud. As General Gordon and his men marched eastward, the mud spattered their uniforms. Having left all extra gear behind to expedite the advance into York county, there was no chance to change his uniform. The mud stained his gray suit.

------

[75] A derogative term used to describe a northerner who sympathized with the Confederacy.

While York was loyal to the Union, not all of its residents were. Some waved enthusiastically at the Confederates from the Tremont House, Washington House, Pete Ahl's, Charles M. Nes, Nett Wickes, and Miss Chapman. Others stood on Democrat Henry Welsh's porch.

George Latimer, a member of a prominent York family, marched with the Gordon's brigade. While others in the Lattimer family were Republicans, George, who had moved from the south, maintained his secessionist views. It was another case where the War Between the States had divided another family.

As General Gordon's brigade marched east, most of the town's people stood outside and gawked at the site of the dirty soldiers. No one fired upon them, and there we no reports of anyone waving the Stars and Stripes at them. Their movement through town remained peaceful.

Some of the Confederates taunted the citizens, with jeers of conquerors. They were thirsty for a Southern victory on Northern soil, which they believed would bring their ultimate independence from the United States. This rag-tag, sweat stained army brought the reality of the Civil War to the streets of York. Now the citizens were witnessing first hand the reality of armed violence and the distinct possibility of battle smoke.

Some of the town's women, although loyal to the Union, fed some of the hungry soldiers. Noticing their youthful, grimy faces, they gave them some bread, which they thankfully accepted.

James Latimer, a young York attorney, kept his family out of sight. He slammed shut the parlor's shutters, and scoffed at his fellow residents that stood outside. Calling it "disgraceful," Latimer felt the resident's of York should have known better.

General Early slept well from Saturday night to Sunday morning. Catching about seven hours of sleep, he was ready for another day's work. The balance of General Early's men had encamped near Big Mount, in western York County, east of East Berlin. Lieutenant Colonel Elijah White's 35th Battalion of Virginia Cavalry encamped miles away, north of Spring Grove.

As he rode toward York via Weigelstown, he saw a man reading a York newspaper. Old Jube asked for it, and the man, sitting on a fence, readily agreed, and handed it over to the Confederate general. He read the newspaper as he rode. It was a source of intelligence for General Early. He would learn of enemy troop movements, and something about the area he was occupying. It was a standard tactic of Civil War generals.

General Early had dispatched most of his cavalry to destroy railroads. The remainder of the 17th Virginia was sent to York Haven to burn the railroad bridges there, and all others south to York. The 35th Virginia Cavalry moved to Hanover Junction, to destroy the railroad bridges there.

Once at York, General Early directed his artillery deployed. On the north side of the town, an artillery battery was positioned on Diehl's Hill. Pointed into York, along the Codorus Creek, the Confederates were ready to fire on the town. All they needed were orders from General Early.

At Weigelstown, General Early had sent the greater part of his cavalry to the mouth of the Conewago to burn two railroad bridges at that point and all others between there and York. Before reaching York, two brigades were ordered into camp about two miles north of the borough near some mills close to the railroad. A brigade under Colonel Avery was moved into town to occupy it, and preserve order. They were quartered in some extensive hospital buildings erected by the United States Government, as well as in the fairgrounds.

"Moving by the way of Weiglestown into the Harrisburg and York road with the other column, I entered the town shortly afterwards, and repeated my instructions to Gordon about the bridge over the Susquehanna, cautioning him to prevent the bridge from being burned if possible," General Early said.[76]

Wearing a faded gray suit, and a worn gray wide-brimmed hat, General Early's beard needed trimmed. Walking with a stoop, he surveyed York from the Centre Square. His dark eyes observed everything.

---

[76] Jubal A. Early Lieutenant General Jubal Anderson Early C. S. A. Autobiographical Sketch and Narrative of The War Between The States, with Notes by R. H. Early. J. B. Lippincott Company, Philadelphia & London, 1912. 259.

General Early walked to David Small's house, just a short distance from the Square, on South George Street. His staff remained outside. The Confederate general shared some refreshments with the Chief Burgess, but soon made it clear why he called upon them.

"I then levied a contribution on the town for 100,000 dollars in money, 2,000 pairs of shoes, 1,000 hats, 1,000 pairs of socks, and three days' rations of all kinds for my troops, for which a requisition was made on the authorities," General Early said.

David Small told General Early that the town could not produce that amount of U.S. cash. To General Early, U.S. dollars had far more value – especially in Pennsylvania. Having thousands of men to provide for, General Early wanted the cash.

But the banks had sent their cash away, David Small told the general.

"What, in such a rich country as this, these people must have laid by immense sums," General Early affirmed. "I am sure you can find it hoarded up in the farmer's canvas bags and housewives' stockings."

"But these hardworking people have not earned their money to give it to you," Chief Burgess Small told General Early. David Small was foolishly provoking a rattlesnake.

General Early told him that he must and would have the money. He ordered a meeting at the courthouse to take up the matter further.

While Burgess Small and General Early talked in the parlor, there was a racket outside. A somewhat nervous Early thought someone was trying to get into the house to take him prisoner. But it was just a soldier that had dropped his rifle.

Relaxing a bit about the commotion outside, General Early left for the courthouse to set up his headquarters.

Another Confederates artillery battery was setup on the south side of York. Position on Webb's hill, the guns pointed north.

York was now under siege. Confederate cannon to the north and south, positioned on the high ground. There was another artillery battery in town, and one was traveling with General

Gordon. Confederate infantry was scattered throughout York. Cavalry moved both north and south of the town, currently on search and destroy mission, tearing up railroad bridges.

In all, about 6,000 Confederate soldiers watched over the borough and its residents, which numbered about 8,500.

Major Granville O. Haller feverishly worked to defend the bridge, and to keep the Confederates from crossing the Susquehanna. Two Napoleon guns and one iron rifle piece were placed in a battery in Columbia. They were positioned to rake the bridge should the Confederates charge across it, especially if the other defenses did not work. The guns were manned by a detachment from the Pennsylvania 27th Militia, under the command of Lieutenant Delaplaine J. Ridgway, and some citizens of Columbia.

Rifle pits were dug and entrenchments were located on the Detwiler farm, located to the south of the York Pike and overlooked the Kreutz Creek, and along the northern outskirts of Wrightsville. They had been widened and deepened.

An elaborate plan was conceived that would drop just one span of the bridge into the Susquehanna. The fourth span (from the Wrightsville side) of the bridge was selected, and mechanics were employed to separate the roof and sides, leaving only "the arches and a very small portion of the lower chords" for crossing over. They bored holes into the arches, and filled them with gunpowder. Fuses were added, and when exploded, it was expected that the timber would splinter, and the span, about 200 feet long, would drop into the river. The drilled holes, gunpowder, and fuses were referred to as mines. It would render the bridge useless to the Confederates. Robert Crane, a local resident and superintendent of the Reading and Columbia Railroad[77], had begun this preparation work a week or so earlier.

McLean Knox of the 9th New York Cavalry, was placed by the mines inserted in the bridge arches. There, Knox was to observe if the enemy approached. He had instructions to order the mines exploded in time to prevent them from getting over the doomed arch.

---

[77] Josiah R. Syphee. History of the Pennsylvania Reserve Corps: A Complete Record of the Organization. (Lancaster, PA: Elias Barr & Co., 1865). Page 447.

Other defenses included the positioning of railroad cars immediately around the entrance of the bridge to cover the retreat of the Federal troops. The cars, loaded with iron ore, were used to barricade the main street leading from York to the bridge. Major Haller ordered the coal and ore hoppers spread out slightly, with narrow intervals to permit infantry to slip between them but close enough together to prevent Confederate cavalry to pass.

Major Haller had directed that the side streets be obstructed by boards piled together to make a complete breastworks for defense by the troops. The piles of lumber barricaded the main intersections of the east and west streets. This work was performed by the citizens of Wrightsville under the directions of Samuel H. Mann, the provost marshal of Wrightsville. Haller had setup the lines of defense to Mann.

About 50 of the 26th Pennsylvania Militia, near exhaustion by their retreat from Gettysburg, guarded the bridgehead. There was also a small guard at the bridge, made up from the 27th Pennsylvania Militia.

Major Haller was also concerned about the natural terrain near Wrightsville.

"About three-fourths of a mile in front of the bridge is a ridge which curves in toward the Susquehanna River, and on the upper side, near the river, beyond this, is another height, both of which are good positions for defense against infantry and cavalry," Major Haller said. "Two small creeks run at the foot of these eminences. But outside of these, above and below Wrightsville, are ridges making in at right angles to the river which, with artillery, would command these defenses."

Major Haller was shorthanded. With the force at his command, it was impossible for him to place troops on the nearby ridges.

"To defend the bridge successfully, these ridges would have to be occupied by our troops, supported by artillery. It would have required, perhaps, five times our number to have garrisoned the line extending from the upper to the lower ridge."

The defense that Major Haller established was to protect the bridge against Confederate cavalry and infantry. But General Gordon had four pieces of artillery with his brigade. Major Haller had no artillery.

The defenders at Wrightsville waited for the Confederates in the warm summer day. Most definitely, they realized the Southerners would be coming down the York-Wrightsville Pike. So far, there was no sign of them.

They would not have to wait much longer.

At 2:00 p.m. Sunday afternoon, June 28, 1863, General Early ordered the bell atop the county courthouse rung. It was the standard way to call a meeting.

Chief Burgess David Small and an assortment of other town leaders and businesspeople filed into the courtroom. County Judge Robert Fisher sat in the audience, and watched as the Confederate General took his seat, on his chair, behind the bench.

There was a hush in the courtroom.

Wearing his faded gray uniform, the man with the scraggly beard looked over his audience. His dark eyes pierced through everyone, watching them much like a barn owl. Finally, he spoke.

"I have taken possession of your town, by authority of the Confederate government," General Early announced.

He told those gathered that the town was safe. Private property would remain protected. His guards were on duty to watch over public buildings. Taverns were closed. But his men needed food and clothing. And he intended to get it.

He produced two requisitions. One was for clothing. He demanded 2,000 pairs of shoes or boots, 1,000 pairs of socks, and 1,000 felt hats. The other requisitioned 21,000 pounds of bacon or pork, 1,200 pounds of salt, 300 gallons of molasses, 1,650 pounds of coffee, 3,500 pounds of sugar, and 28,000 pounds of baked bread or 165 barrels of flour. The food requisition was to be filled by 4:00 p.m.

General Early demanded this requisitions be filled at once, and if the town did not comply, his Confederate soldiers would enter the town's stores and houses and seize the items. And he wanted the cash.

When General Early finally stopped talking, David Small stood and objected to the demands. The chief burgess repeated what he had told the general in private a short time ago. The banks holdings and the store's supplies have been sent east, prior to General Early's arrival.

Members of the Committee of Safety stood and agreed with David Small.

General Early was not persuaded. "Then I shall have to take the hats from your heads, and shoes from your feet, and the coasts from your backs, for I must have them, and I must have some money, too," he said.

The general stood, looked at everyone, turned, and abruptly left the dusty courtroom. The community leaders immediately huddled to decide what to do next. They quickly appointed collectors, and dispatched them to the town's five wards. Certificates would be given to each person providing donates supplies or funds. There were still a few hours to collect the food the general had requisitioned.

A short time later, Major C.E. Snodgrass sent Chief Burgess David Small a written message. "Sir, General Early directs me to ascertain whether or not the requisition by me will be filled."

If Major Snodgrass's inquiry was designed to keep the pressure on the town, it worked. The townspeople were busy collecting money.

Some the residents turned over all they had. Others refused, and gave little, or nothing. James Latimer had $200, but only turned over $100. When totaled, the town raised about $28,600. It was far less than the amount the cantankerous Confederate General Early had demanded.

His supply officers received a small portion of the money to buy cattle. Pennsylvania farmers parted with their livestock much more readily if they were handed U.S. dollars, rather than Confederate money.

The P.A. & S. Small Company provided all of the food General Early demanded. It was enough for about three days worth of rations for the Confederates. The Confederates paid the Small Company about $1,200 – in Confederate dollars – for the food supplies. Undoubtedly, the Small family faced certain financial ruin if the town was fired. The company owned and operated several mills. A report had been received where the Confederates had destroyed one of his mills. General Early checked, then rechecked the report. It proved false. If the mill had been intentionally destroyed, General Early had issued orders that the soldier torching the property would be immediately executed.

The Smalls turned over large quantities of flour that was transported to the bakery at the federal hospital in southern York. The borough's residents provided the Confederates with 1200 to 1500 pairs of shoes. They were taken from the shelves – including those that were dropped off for repair.

Still, the disposition of the Confederate general was tested. He was not happy with the amount of money he had received. General Early's soldiers were happy and contented that Sunday afternoon. They filled their bellies with fresh roast beef and hot bread. It was a great Sunday for the gray and butternut clad soldiers strategically positioned in York.

For the moment, everything seemed to be working out. The Confederates occupied the town. York, a kaleidoscope of residential and commercial buildings of all sorts, was a true 1860's American city. It was the county seat, and bustled with commerce from farm and manufacturing production. On this Sunday, the townspeople were coping, and the soldiers were not destroying any private or public property or molesting anyone. General Early turned his main attention away from the current demands he had placed on York, and focused on the huge military prize that was just 12 miles east of him.

The Pennsylvania Historic Marker located in Wrightsville at the present-day Rt. 462 bridge.

Chapter 7
The Rebels Are
In Wrightsville

As Confederate General Gordon advanced toward Wrightsville, he kept mulling over the contents of that note that was handed to him in the bouquet of flowers by the young girl.

Having moved his men east on the Lancaster pike, he encamped near the Old York Valley Inn. His men were most probably thinking they had finished an easy day's march. The thoughts of a relaxed lunch, some productive foraging, and full night's sleep danced in their heads. Few could have realized that they were resting along a pathway established long before by Indians, long before the arrival of European settlers. Widened into the Monocacy Trail in 1739, the York pike connected to the site of the old Wright's Ferry.

Ironically, it was this road that the members of the Continental Congress used when fleeing the British. Their Southern forefathers, who were members of the Congress, traveled that same road. Having used Anderson's Ferry, located just north of Columbia near Chickies Rock at Marietta to cross the Susquehanna, the members of the Continental Congress met in York in 1777 and 1778, some 85 years earlier.

General Gordon stopped at the Smyser house, located a few miles east of York, on the estate and farm was known as The Cedars. Daniel Smyser had died in 1862. Mrs. Smyser and two relatives prepared a fine meal for the Confederate. Just before he left for Wrightsville, he told Mrs. Smyser to report any property loss to him.

Albert Smyser, her 18-year-old son, did just that. His horse was gone. General Gordon ordered his aide to find the horse, and return it to Albert.

At some point early that afternoon, General Gordon rode back to York. There, his commander, General Early, reissued his desire to capture and secure the Wrightsville-Columbia Bridge. This was a direct deviation from General Early's commander and his initial order. Confederate General Richard "Dick" Ewell, whose troops were moving toward Harrisburg, had ordered the bridge destroyed. General Early was hell-bent on cutting the Pennsylvania Central Railroad, marching on Lancaster, and forcing a hefty contribution to the Southern cause from the residents. Then he would move on to Harrisburg from the southeast. General Early was optimistic, and quite typical of the advancing Confederates. There was no real resistance to the movement of the Confederate army. York's capitulation afforded General Early sufficient time to launch his unauthorized trek on Lancaster.

Having again received his directions from General Early, General Gordon rode out of York, and returned to his troops sometime that mid-afternoon. He ordered them to march eastward.

General Gordon and his column moved toward Wrightsville. He was in command of 1,800 stalwart men. They were easily capable of marching 15 miles a day, and frequently marched further on some days.

To his front was Wrightsville, and well-thought out defense, manned by an inferior force of mostly militia and recent volunteers. The most experienced men were sick or wounded invalids that left the York Military Hospital to defend the river town. The entire defensive force had been hurriedly assembled and inadequately trained. Yet they remained in their trenches, prepared to defend that key bridge that spanned the Susquehanna. General Gordon's professional soldiers were experienced, battle-hardened, and spirited, and overwhelmingly outnumbered Wrightsville's defenders.

All day, the town was on edge. Wrightsville's churches had cancelled their regular Sunday services. The preacher cancelled

Sunday school. Some of the churches managed to hold morning prayer meetings. The borough's defenders readied for an attack. They dug their trenches deeper.

Major Haller and Colonel Frick had been busy directing every defensive measure they could think of to protect the town and the bridge. They knew their force, which numbered between 1,200 to 1,400 men, was too thin to stop a Confederate infantry attack. Without artillery, they knew that they probably could not stop the Southerners. Having military experience, both commanders knew that their defensive trenches were susceptible to artillery attack. From the high ground near Wrightsville, the Confederates could lob shells down on their men. Using the nearby high ridges, the Southerners could shatter the town's defense.

General Gordon stopped his column, rode his mount to the high ground at Strickler's Hill, and studied the Federal positions. He was about three-quarters of a mile in front of them. He soon agreed that the best way to approach them was to the right of the Union defenders, just as the unexplained note in the flower bouquet had suggested.

"I eagerly scanned the prospect with my field-glasses, in order to verify the truth of the mysterious communication or detect its misrepresentations," General Gordon said. "There, in full view before us, was the town, just as described, nestling on the banks of the Susquehanna. There was the blue line of soldiers guarding the approach, drawn up, as indicated, along an intervening ridge and across the pike. There was the long bridge spanning the Susquehanna and connecting the town with Columbia on the other bank."

As General Gordon peered through his binoculars, looking toward the bridge, seeing the Federal blue line, it must have been an exciting sight for him on that late Sunday afternoon. There, in front of him, was the big prize. The longest covered bridge in America, at a strategic location, positioned across the ever-moving Susquehanna, lay within his grasp. He had to feel the excitement. It was just beyond the slope in Wrightsville.

The bridge was grand. President James Buchanan made the bridge famous just four years earlier. It was widely reported that Pennsylvania's only resident to become President took a terrible tumble on the bridge. The President fell while following his usual practice of walking the mile-long bridge between Wrightsville and Columbia. The president regularly departed from his Lancaster-bound train to stretch his legs. On one trip, he turned to speak to several York County acquaintances. He then tripped over an obstruction. The fall stunned the chief executive. After a few minutes, he was able to continue his walk to Columbia. He then proceeded by rail to his Lancaster home that he called Wheatland. All was reported well with the president. He returned through York "in excellent health and fine spirits," one newspaper reported.

To General Gordon, what was the most important fact of all about the Columbia-Wrightsville Bridge, was the deep gorge or ravine running off to the right and extending around the left flank of the Federal line and to the river below the bridge. General Gordon realized there was "not an inaccurate detail in that note" handed to him by the young girl a few hours earlier in the center York.

"I did not hesitate, therefore, to adopt its suggestion of moving down the gorge in order to throw my command on the flank, or possibly in the rear, of the Union troops and force them to a rapid retreat or surrender," General Gordon said. "The result of this movement vindicated the strategic wisdom of my unknown and—judging by the handwriting—woman correspondent, whose note was none the less martial because embedded in roses."

General Gordon observed the extent of Wrightsville and the nature of the surrounding ground. The geography had required Major Haller to establish a defense over one mile in length.

To garrison this line, Colonel J. G. Frick's 27th Pennsylvania Militia (excluding the artillery and bridge guards) were used. There were 650 men in position. The York Battalion, which included invalids and the Patapsco Guards, were 238 in number. Lieutenant-Colonel William H. Sickles positioned three companies of the 20th Pennsylvania Militia, which was 200 men. The number of men assigned to defend Wrightsville and the bridge totaled 1,088.

The Federal troops were positioned in various defensive positions. The 27th Pennsylvania Militia, with Colonel Frick Commanding, occupied the rifle-pits in front and on both sides the York Pike. The company of Black soldiers from Columbia was positioned with the 27th Pennsylvania. One company was thrown forward on the pike to picket the road.

The York Battalion, which consisted of soldiers, some wounded, and convalescents, was placed under command the command of Lieutenant-Colonel Green, 27th Pennsylvania Militia. They were posted on the left of Colonel Frick's regiment, extending to the Susquehanna River, with the Patapsco Guards in reserve. These men, who had been under fire, although older or wounded, were place in a strategic position. This line was most likely to be seriously assaulted, as the ground there most favored the enemy's approach. The battalion of 20th Pennsylvania Militia, with Lieutenant Colonel Sickles commanding, guarded the approaches on the right of the 27th Pennsylvania Militia to the river. There were about 200 men in the 20th Pennsylvania.

What remained of Captain Bell's Adams County Cavalry was sent forward on the York pike and neighboring heights to scout and ascertain if the enemy approached, and their probable force. About a dozen were sent forward to observe the Old Baltimore Road. The Philadelphia City Troop, under the command of Samuel J. Randall, patrolled Wrightsville, and obliged every soldier to remain with his company. Several from the Philadelphia City Troop were selected as messengers. They were stationed with the field officers to carry communications.

Major Haller knew the Confederates were approaching Wrightsville. Scouts were making regular reports of the advancement of General Gordon's brigade. Major Haller's scouts had already gleaned information that York was occupied at 10 a. m. by 1,000 rebels. Two things Major Haller did not know was the actual size of General Gordon's force, or that he was moving toward them with artillery.

A detachment from the 27th Pennsylvania and about 50 exhausted militia that were with Major Haller since General Early entered Gettysburg guarded the entrance of the bridge.

"There was reason to hope that their number was not formidable, and we might save the bridge," Major Haller said.

By mid-afternoon, another scout galloped into Wrightsville. He reported that the Confederates were halfway between York and Wrightsville. Messages were sent to Colonel Frick, who had crossed over to Columbia. He too was informed of the rapidly approaching Southerners. The Philadelphia City Troop patrolled the streets of Wrightsville, delivering communications among the commanders, and checking on the defensive positions.

Reports were also received by Major Haller of the successes of the Confederate cavalry working in the southern end of York County. The reports of their destruction of the railroad bridges and telegraph lines also reached Colonel Frick. The military commanders called their troops to arms. Only the hardiest of Wrightsville residents remained in their homes. The ringing of the bells summoned everyone to alert. The flow of refugees across the covered bridge had nearly ended.

General Couch was greatly concerned about the situation along the Susquehanna. He sent a message to Colonel Frick on June 28th.

"York has surrendered. Our troops will fall back from there to Wrightsville to-night. If Major Haller is with them, he is my aide-de-camp. Have reliable men sent down to the Conowingo Bridge. Impress horses, and send good officers or volunteers. The commanding officer will take up planks, and in no event should that bridge fall into enemy's hands, or any fords. Tell the people of Lancaster that the time has come for action. Have all boats and rafts along the river brought on this side."[78]

General Couch clearly recognized how serious it was to keep General Early and his Confederates from crossing the Susquehanna.

---

[78] United States War Department. The War of the Rebellion: a Compilation of the Official Records of the Union and Confederate Armies, 1880-1891. Chapter XXXIX, Part III, Page 385.

From his elevated position, General Gordon planned the assault on Wrightsville. He wanted to capture the mile-long bridge.

"As my orders were not restricted, except to direct me to cross the Susquehanna, if possible, my immediate object was to move rapidly down that ravine to the river, then along its right bank to the bridge, seize it, and cross to the Columbia side," General Gordon explained years later. "Once across, I intended to mount my men, if practicable, so as to pass rapidly through Lancaster in the direction of Philadelphia, and thus compel General Meade to send a portion of his army to the defense of that city."

It was around 5:00 p.m. when General Gordon peered through his field-glasses at the blue Union line. He observed their defense of Wrightsville. General Gordon decided that the best approach was to the right, along the railroad that ran down creek in a deepening ravine. In this way, his force could work its way to a jump off position on the Federals southern flank. With some luck, he might move through the ravine unobserved. With a sudden rush, his men could get between the Union defenders and the bridge. Then he could capture it. He also decided to test the northern flank of the Federal blue line. He had enough gray coats to pressure both sides of the defender's horseshoe–shaped line.

General Gordon started the work of crushing the Wrightsville defense slowly and deliberately. He was confident that his men could easily defeat the local militia. He wanted to get between them and the bridge, so that they could not retreat across it, and then set it on fire. He decided to use the deep ravine caused by the Kreutz Creek that flowed to the Susquehanna south of the bridge.

Using his cavalry, General Gordon positioned his men along the south side of Wrightsville. In the mix, he threw some infantry, while the remainder of his force marched toward the town on the Wrightsville-York Pike. There were rolling fields of golden wheat, about waist-high, between him and the town. The wheat waved in the afternoon breeze. It provided good cover for armed men. At the point where the Confederates were in rifle range of the defenders, they fanned out into the wheat.

Colonel Frick had sent what remaining forces he had in Columbia across the bridge. He hoped to defend the bridge until reinforcements could arrive. He had learned that General Dix was in route from Philadelphia with additional forces.

The day before, Colonel Frick had sent four companies from Columbia across the bridge. One of those companies was a Negro company. Three companies from Columbia had returned to their homes earlier on Sunday, probably to defend their families and properties should the Southerners get across the bridge. Most likely, these companies consisted of men that had volunteered earlier, and were relieved by the Pennsylvania Emergency Militia.

The defenders strengthened their defenses. They dug their holes deeper and wider. They worked in the summer heat while ready for an attack. The only Columbia company that remained was the one made up of Black soldiers. It was that company and Colonel's Frick's Emergency militia that did the dirty, hard work of digging the defensive trenches deeper and wider. Throughout the day, the women of Wrightsville fed the sweaty men protecting their little borough.

The defenders had formed what looks like a great "U" set sideways on the map. By midday Sunday, between 1,200 and 1,400 mostly raw militia were deployed around Wrightsville in this "U" defense. The bottom of the "U" was positioned on the nearest, highest ground west of Wrightsville. The line was about 2800 yards long. The bottom of the line was about 400 yards wide, where it crossed the York pike. It stretched back about 1200 yards to the Susquehanna. Typically, a force of 1,200 men defend a line of only 400 yards. It was just too big a line – nearly a mile and half long – and not near enough men. The line to the south sloped out of effective musket range, toward Kreutz Creek, and the railroad flanked east toward the river. On the north side, a wooded hill line existed[79]. To protect these features would have required a longer line, and the defenders spread even thinner.

And that was the simple problem facing Major Haller and Colonel Frick. The line was too long and guarded by too few men. Both Haller and Frick knew they could only hold the line against a small force of cavalry. And they knew the approaching force was much larger.

Captain Bell's cavalry galloped back within the line. The Black troops put down their shovels and axes, and picked up their

---

[79] This is where modern day Route 30 is now located.

muskets. There were 53 Blacks on duty in the trenches in Wrightsville[80]. Word quickly spread that many Rebels were heading their way. The Black troops remained throughout the skirmish, only retreating when ordered to do so.[81]

When the first shots rang out, it was around 5:30 p.m. Captain Strickler had positioned men across the turnpike as pickets to guard the approaches from the Confederates. The Southerners, with far superior numbers, went about the work of flanking defenders. With rifle fire, it was easy to move the pickets back toward Wrightsville.

"The enemy advanced very slowly, feeling their way, and occasionally firing, which our men returned," said Major Haller. "The luxuriant grain in the fields in our front and the woods on our left covered the assailants, while our rifle-pits protected our men; hence the firing did but little injury."

Some of the Southerners moved toward the southeast, along the railroad line, then disappeared into the gulch were Kreutz Creek was. The two sides exchanged shots on the slopes of the Detwiler farm. The Confederates were doing their best to move along in a stealthy advancement. They could not be seen in the wheat fields until they would stand up to fire their rifles. The Federal defenders remained in their trenches. The Confederates caused no casualties.

This movement of the Confederates lasted for about an hour. Colonel Frick noticed another enemy force of suddenly emerge from the woods on Hellam Hills, north of his position. Using the woods as cover, the wily Confederates had worked themselves within three hundred yards of the Susquehanna. Now the South-

---

[80] Lancaster Examiner & Herald, July 1, 1863, Page 2, Column 4.

[81] This was later acknowledged in Colonel Frick's Official Report. He said, "Before closing this report, justice compels me to make mention of the excellent conduct of the company of negroes from Columbia. After working industriously in the rifle-pits all day, when the fight commenced they took their guns and stood up to their work bravely. They fell back only when ordered to do so."

erners were threatening both of his flanks – to the north and south.

Rifle fire had increased in intensity. Major Haller ordered the drum corps to the bridge. He also ordered all the citizens of Wrightsville to take immediate refuge behind a stone or brick wall. Many fled to their cellars.

The Philadelphia City Troop slowly withdrew toward the bridge, as did the Gettysburg Cavalry, under the command of Captain Bell. Heavy rifle fire to the south indicated that the Confederates were advancing along the railroad line on the left flank.

Colonel Frick knew what this meant. The Confederates, when they made their charge, would cut him and his men off from the bridge. It was time to withdraw across the bridge.

At 6:50 p.m., the front line of the defenders delivered a volley of heavy fire on the Southerners. They then began pulling back, toward the bridge.

The Confederates used their artillery, and began shelling the town. They had moved a battery to within 500 yards of the bridge's tollgate, placing one section on the pike, and another on the side. Colonel Frick withdrew his forces, pulling in his flanks. At 6:57 p.m., a Confederate shell whizzed overhead and burst over Wrightsville. Shrapnel fell to the ground. That hastened the defender's retreat.

At first, they were trying to hit defenders in their trenches. One did, decapitating a Black soldier[82]. As the Federals withdrew, the Confederates artillerymen increased the range of their cannons. No doubt they were trying to hit the Federals who were on the move, but their shells missed the intended target. One shell hit a Federal captain in the leg. He hid in Joshua Issac's home until the next day. He died from the wound the next day. He was Robert B. March, a Philadelphian[83].

---

[82] The name of this Black volunteer remains unknown. There is no primary citation available that records his identity. It is likely that he was buried in Columbia, at the Zion Hill Cemetery, located at the corner of 5th Street and Chiques Hill Road. Other Black troops that served with the famed 54th Massachusetts are buried in this once neglected cemetery.
[83] Nye, Wilbur S. *Here Come the Rebels!* Louisiana State University Press, Baton Rouge, LA, 1963. 293-294.

The Confederate shelling did not do any serious property damage. As their shells exploded in the streets of Wrightsville, the residents remained in their cellars. Using four Confederate artillery pieces, W.A. Tanner's battery lobbed over both solid and exploding shells. The Confederate artillerymen fired about 40 shells.[84] Some of the Southerner's shells fell into the river.

Others hit some of the houses in Wrightsville. The Ferry House, also called the Big Brick Hotel, was hit by a Confederate shell, damaging its first floor. A second shell smashed through to the second floor, rolled around, but did not explode. It was later said that some area residents had wished the Confederate shell had exploded, because it was there, on the second floor, where the prohibitionists regularly met to discuss how to stop alcohol consumption in the borough of Wrightsville.

One shell fell dangerously close to Amanda Beaverson and her two children. Another shell crashed into James Kerr Smith's house, located at Forth and Hellam Streets. The Confederates shell smashed into his wall. In the cellars, the town's residents hovered in fear and fright, wondering if the Confederates shells would level their homes and the town burned to ashes. The Confederates did not try to hit the bridge with their artillery.

Joseph H. Black, a Columbia resident, said, "They were shelling the town but not the bridge; they did not want that burned."[85]

From General Gordon's position on Strickler's Hill, he could not see the Columbia-Wrightsville Bridge. The houses in Wrightsville obstructed his vision. The bank dropped off sharply to the Susquehanna, making it impossible to see the area of the bridgehead.

The Confederates shelling had the desired effect. It forced the defenders from their entrenchments. Fresh, untrained, without any battle experience, the troops believe it better to retreat than to have Confederates grenades dropped on them. They started their retreat across the bridge.

---

[84] General Early, years later, wrote that defenders at Wrightsville started running after the third shell. This suggests a number of artillery shells far less than 40.

[85] From Joseph H. Black's sworn deposition made on August 19, 1904, before Henry B. Bruner, Notary Public.

The citizens of Columbia had gathered and sought strategic vantage points to watch the action, and see what was going on. It did not get much more exciting than this. The only thing that separated them from the Rebels was the mile-wide Susquehanna. All the gray suits had to do was march across the grand bridge. Of course, they had to control it first. The hill rising to the northwest out of Columbia filled with spectators and the curious. On what is modern day Third Street in the Borough of Columbia, the area lined with people watching the events in the distance. Some watched from porches, rooftops, or from climbing trees. Others congregated on the Mt. Bethel grounds, at Second and Walnut Streets. Some were closer to the river. They all watched and waited. The question on everyone's mind was "can we stop the Confederates?"

The defenders withdrew toward the bridge. They moved between the small spaces between the ore cars that were positioned as a barricade against the Confederate cavalry. For the most part, their withdrawal was orderly. The officers maintain discipline among their inexperienced troops. Under Confederate fire, they moved back to the bridge. The troops marched across the bridge, in order, and reassembled in front of their company colors in Columbia. From there, they marched to their encampment.

All of the defender's troops, except Lt. Colonel Sickles' men from the 20th Pennsylvania, successfully retreated. For the most part, the withdrawal was orderly. As the Confederates pushed forward, some retreated in haste. Confused, inexperienced, and under fire, they ran to the safety of the bridge. Those men would be mentioned later in Major Haller's official report about the incident. He wrote, "I regret to have to add that the conduct of Colonel Sickles and two companies of the Twentieth Pennsylvania Militia deserves investigation. It has been represented to me that the lieutenant colonel and some 15 or 20 of his men have unnecessarily, but deliberately, surrendered to the Confederate troops. Some of the men threw away their arms, and the two companies, without authority, hurried away from Columbia, straggling along the road to Lancaster and filling the country with alarming reports."

In Columbia, the Wrightsville defenders emerged from the long square box. The troops filed onto the street, and reassembled by company in proper order. They had held off the Confederate's advance a little more than an hour. Despite their inexperience, and the bombardment from the Southern artillery, the men did well. The small group of civilian workers, who had entered the bridge per military orders hours before, were not with the Wrightsville's defenders. The blue coats that were invalids wobbled out of the bridge. They had returned fire in Wrightsville, as best they could. Colonel Frick's men had used the bridge for retreat, and left it standing.

It was nearly dark when the Confederate infantry swarmed into town, filling the streets with a sea of gray and butternut coats. Obviously tired from the 20-mile march of that day, the Southerners ran toward the bridgehead. By now, all except 19 of the defenders had crossed the bridge, retreating to make a stand in Columbia. Nineteen laid down their rifles and surrendered to the Confederates. Captain Bell's Adams County Cavalry rode into town from a scouting mission, and encountered hordes of Confederates. They turned and retreated. One trooper went down when his horse was shot from under him. He hid in a house to avoid capture by the Rebels. Captain Bell's Cavalry later crossed the Susquehanna further down the river.

Few were emerging from the bridge, as most stood in Columbia. The citizens that had assembled cheered the uniformed men. It was time to make the bridge useless to the Confederates.

Major Haller was back in Columbia, organizing a defense of the river town. Should the Southerners break through and cross the covered bridge, Major Haller was determined to fight the advancing Confederates in the Borough's streets.

Major Haller also had orders from General Couch. "When you find it necessary to withdraw the main body of Col. Frick's command from Wrightsville, leave a proper number on the other side to destroy the bridges and use your own discretion in their destruction. Keep them open as long as possible with prudence."

Local resident Robert Crane had returned to the bridge earlier that day. He was one of several civilians that stood by to receive orders from the military commanders. Another of the other local civilians that stayed on the bridge was John Q. Denny, who lived about a mile from Columbia. He was one of the carpenters engaged by Robert Crane.

Having received orders earlier from Major Haller, Robert Crane had employed "a force of carpenters and bridge-builders for the purpose of cutting and throwing a span."[86] The bridge guards had permitted them access to the bridge under the orders of Colonel Frick. A team of nineteen carpenters were hired to do the work. They had taken up the floor, cut timbers, and loaded the bridges arches "for the purpose of throwing down a span of the bridge in case the rebels came to the bridge."[87]

The work crew had bored arches, and the holes filled with gunpowder. Four men had been placed in charge of the fuses. In addition to Denny, there were John Lockhard, Jacob Rich, and Jacob Miller.

The Confederates pressed toward the bridgehead. The last of the defenders stepped onto it from the Wrightsville shore. Major Charles McLean Knox had positioned himself on the Columbia-Wrightsville Bridge so he could see if Confederates were approaching the bridgehead. From his vantage point, he could see the steep hill, and if the Confederates were descending it. Suddenly, they were there.

It was Major Knox, who around 7:30 p.m., ordered the fuses lit and the mines on the bridge arches exploded. He had received agreement from Colonel Frick to give the order. It was a perfect, well-conceived plan. The fourth span from the Wrightsville side of the bridge would rapidly crash into the Susquehanna. It would instantly stop any advancement of the hordes of Confederates.

---

[86] United States War Department. The War of the Rebellion: a Compilation of the Official Records of the Union and Confederate Armies, 1880-1891. Chapter XXXIX, Part III, Page 410.
[87] From John Q. Denny's sworn deposition made on August 19, 1904, before Henry. B. Bruner, Notary Public.

"All the forces having passed over from the borough of Wrightsville, the plank flooring was removed and the match applied to the fuse," Robert Crane said.

"When the rebels appeared at the entrance to the bridge, the order was given by the commanding officer to light the fuse," confirmed.

"Every charge was perfect and effective," said Robert Crane.

With the fuses lit, the cord burnt. Then there was an explosion. The bridge rattled, rocked, and shook. The arches at the fourth span cracked and splinted. When the dust and dirt settled, and the smoke cleared, the bridge remained intact. The span near Wrightsville did not fall into the river. The bridge could hold the advancing Confederates as they crossed the Susquehanna.

From the eastern shore, the onlookers in Columbia wondered what had happened. They heard the faint explosion that rumbled through the bridge. But it looked like nothing really occurred. The Confederate's artillery rounds were louder, distinct.

"It simply splintered the arch; scarcely shook the bridge," Denny recalled. Even though the bridge had been weakened, and wood removed, "all excepting the arches and a very small portion of the lower chords" the mighty covered bridge stood.

Four strategically bored holes filled with powder splintered the arches, but the weakened span remained stretched across the stone pillars. No one could deny that early Pennsylvanian's knew how to build a bridge to defy Mother Nature. Here was proof of the extensive skill of the craftsmen that dangled above the flowing Susquehanna to build the grandest covered bridge. Rumbling railroad cars could not shake it apart. They built a bridge so strong and structurally sound that Union mines burrowed into its arches could not destroy it.

Despite the explosion, he Confederates swarmed toward the bridge-head. They prepared to cross the covered bridge, and enter Columbia.

When the bridge mines only splintered the wooden arch, and did not drop the fourth span from Wrightsville into the Susquehanna, the military commander knew what had to be done. He ordered the bridge set afire.

"It was then that I felt it to be my duty, in order to prevent the enemy from crossing the river and marching on to Harrisburg in the rear, destroying on his route railroads and bridges, to order the bridge to be set on fire," Colonel Frick said.

"When it was observed that so little damage was done by the explosion, we were ordered to set fire to the bridge, which we did, I myself being one to assist in the operation," Denny said.

Colonel Frick had given the order. The men started the fire. Earlier, the work crew had saturated the floor near the Wrightsville side of the covered bridge with some crude oil from a small Columbia refinery. This fueled the flames, and they spread rapidly through the structure. Major Knox, Denny, Crane, and the rest of the work party rapidly crossed the bridge, heading toward Columbia. Their pace quickened as they saw the flames engulf the weakened span, and began spreading in each direction.

For about fifteen minutes, there had been only a quiet, nervous calm. The Confederate cannon were silent. There were no rifle shots. It was eerie. Confederate soldiers had entered the bridge from the western shore.

The onlookers in Columbia noticed the fire, at first small, near the Wrightsville side of the bridge.

"They've done it!" somebody in the crowd shouted. They cheered as the flames became more visible. Down winds spread the blaze.

In a short time, the breezes were whipping the fire that raced toward both ends of the covered bridge. Sparks, flames, and thick smoke rose in evening darkness. The work crew, having reached Columbia, turned and watched the destruction of the bridge. In minutes, the fire spread rapidly. It was all consuming, and totally out of control.

Some of the Confederate advance guard ran out of the western side of bridge. They had entered, hovering on the sides, awaiting backups, before crossing. Using their blankets, they tried to slap out the fire. But it was far too little too late. The fire roared out of control. They had to retreat, or become engulfed in the roaring flames.

From every viewpoint in Wrightsville, Columbia, and all surrounding places, there was a great fire on the river. It consumed the bridge, brightening the dark night with tall flames and sparks that rose toward the summer sky. Heat from the massive, self-consuming fire was felt on both shores of the Susquehanna. Essentially a long square box resting on stone pillars, it was a perfect structure to feed a fire. With both ends open, the flames lived on the air supply swooping in from each sides. Down winds and up winds whipped the flames into a frenzy. The major transportation connection across the Susquehanna was totally engulfed in uncontrollable fire. There was nothing but a great wall of flame. The roar of the fire grew in intensity. Flames danced high into the sky, and down to the river surface.

In Columbia, the Washington Hotel on Front Street, became a point of observation.

"There was a fine view from the top (of) porch," Hugh M. North recalled[88]. North was a local attorney, and practiced law in Columbia. He was the solicitor of the Columbia Bank, the owner of the bridge[89]. "That was well filled by citizens, men and women…"

Attorney North was just one of thousands that watched the flames rise across the Susquehanna that early summer Sunday evening. The spectacle lasted for hours. The well-seasoned lumber and timbers sparked and hissed hours. Flames rose hundreds of feet off the river. Black smoke billowed, but was not seen because of the night's darkness. The fire burned and heaved, engulfing the entire length of the bridge.

"I was in that company and I stayed from about 7 o'clock, or before the fire began until it was totally destroyed, which took over four hours," North said.

On the eastern side, the Columbia Fire Companies tried to save their side of the bridge, but their effort was useless. The flames too fierce, the fire too intense, there was nothing that could be done to save any portion of the bridge. Some soldiers joined in with the firemen to stop the fire. Using axes, the hacked away at

---

[88] From Hugh M. North's sworn deposition made August 19, 1904, before Henry B. Bruner, Notary Public.
[89] Originally chartered the Columbia Bridge Company, then the Columbia Bank and Bridge Company, the corporation changed names again to Columbia Bank before 1863. In 1864, the Columbia Bank changed names to the Columbia National Bank, to comply with U.S. banking laws.

the timber, all in an useless effort to eliminate fuel for the mass inferno. Their plan did not work. The only thing to do was guard against flying embers, and prevent the flames from the bridge to spread to any structure in town. Clouds of smoke, filled with sparks and embers, billowed into the sky.

In Wrightsville, the Confederates hoped to save the burning bridge. They used blankets and tools to try to stop the fire.

"With great energy my men labored to save the bridge," General Gordon said. "I called on the citizens of Wrightsville for buckets and pails, but none were to be found."[90]

The Confederates had feverishly tried to collect pails and buckets, tools, and any other firefighting equipment. There was none to be found. Even the town's fire engine was missing. The residents of Wrightsville claimed that the Federals had carried all such items away. The Southerners had no chance of extinguishing the massive blaze.

The fire spread back from the bridge to Wrightsville.

General Gordon ordered two regiments to form a bucket brigade. The line stretched to the Susquehanna. As the town itself was threatened, and sparks landed on the roofs of some buildings, miraculously buckets filled with water suddenly appeared.

"There was, however, no lack of buckets and pails a little later, when the town was on fire," General Gordon said.

"The bridge might burn, for that incommoded, at the time, only the impatient Confederates, and these Pennsylvanians were not in sympathy with my expedition, nor anxious to facilitate the movement of such unwelcome visitors. But when the burning bridge fired the lumber-yards on the river's banks, and the burning lumber fired the town, buckets and tubs and pails and pans innumerable came from their hiding-places, until it seemed that, had the whole of Lee's army been present, I could have armed them with these implements to fight the rapidly spreading flames," General Gordon later wrote.

Citizens joined the gray coats in fighting the fire. Reluctant at first, the threat of the entire town burning to the ground forced the townspeople to fight the fire along side the Confederates. Together, buckets passed from hand to hand to fight the fire.

---

[90] John B. Gordon, Reminiscences of The Civil War (New York: Scribner's, 1903), 147.

"My men labored as earnestly and bravely to save the town as they did to save the bridge. In the absence of fire-engines or other appliances, the only chance to arrest the progress of the flames was to form my men around the burning district, with the flank resting on the river's edge, and pass rapidly from hand to hand the pails of water. Thus, and thus only, was the advancing, raging fire met, and at a late hour of the night checked and conquered. There was one point especially at which my soldiers combated the fire's progress with immense energy, and with great difficulty saved an attractive home from burning," General Gordon said.

The roof of the Wrightsville House, 127-129 North Front Street, caught fire. First known as Mansion House, many travelers used this hotel for years after crossing the Susquehanna by ferry or via the bridge. The Confederate soldiers extinguished the roof fire, saving the building.

The flames in Wrightsville were eventually stopped. Together with the Confederate soldiers, the townspeople had worked to save Wrightsville. They succeeded. Much of the town was saved.

Fire destroyed six buildings in Wrightsville. The Kauffelt and Lanius Lumber Yard, the Henry Kauffelt Planning Mill, Wolf's foundry, and three houses owned by G.W. Harris burned. The loss of the buildings at the lumberyard and planning mill was set at $9,000. The loss to the three Harris houses was $4000. The foundry, which was owned by people from Baltimore, was completely destroyed.

The great fire could be seen for miles. Thirty miles to the north, the bridge fire could be seen by people in Harrisburg. To west, in Hanover, also about 30 miles away, the people saw the flames, and thought York was on fire. People in Lancaster saw the rising embers and fire.

One of those that saw it from a distance was none other than General Early.

"I rode in the direction of Wrightsville. By the time I got outside of the town I saw the smoke arising from the burning bridge, and when I reached Wrightsville I found the bridge entirely destroyed, General Early said. "I regretted this very much." [91]

As the Confederate General realized the Columbia-Wrightsville Bridge was in flames, so was his grand plan for capturing the southern portion of Pennsylvania. As the smoke swept skyward, General Early knew his chance of crossing the Susquehanna was gone. "… notwithstanding my orders to destroy the bridge, I had found the country so defenseless, and the militia which Curtin had called into service so utterly inefficient, that I determined to cross the Susquehanna, levy a contribution on the rich town of Lancaster, cut the Central Railroad, and then move up in rear of Harrisburg while General Ewell was advancing against that city from the other side, relying upon being able, in any event that might happen, to mount my division on the horses which had been accumulated in large numbers on the east side of the river, by the farmers who had fled before us, and make my escape by moving to the west of the army, after damaging the railroads and canals on my route as much as possible."

As General Early rode toward Wrightsville, the glow of the great fire on the river became clearer. His grand dream of capturing the bridge, invading Lancaster, and approaching Harrisburg from the eastern shore of Susquehanna was gone. What was left of the plan was falling into the Susquehanna. The smell of the burning embers filled the air. It was thick with the unmistakable odor of burning wood.

For four hours, the Columbia-Wrightsville Bridge burned, and pieces fell into the river. The logs and timber dropped into the river, and floated away. It was an impressive, rolling fire. There was no controlling it. At this point, it would burn as long as it wanted. In a way, the fire became a massive, living monster. It burned the transportation connector as it chose.

---

[91] Jubal A. Early, Lieutenant General Jubal Anderson Early C. S. A. Autobiographical Sketch and Narrative of The War Between The States, with Notes by R. H. Early. J. B. Lippincott Company, Philadelphia & London, 1912. Page 260-261.

Many thought the river was on fire. The embers and ash and smoke and flames rose a hundred feet into the night air. The fire hissed and spit. The heat was intense.

General Early and General Gordon spoke. General Early ordered General Gordon to return to York the next day. General Early headed back to York, his plans to cross the Susquehanna thwarted. But there was still the issue of the bounty to be paid by the York citizens.

"By the time I got outside of the town I saw the smoke arising from the burning bridge, and when I reached Wrightsville I found the bridge entirely destroyed," General Early said.

General Early believed in his plan. He said, "This scheme, in which I think I could have been successful, was, however, thwarted by the destruction of the bridge, as there was no other means of crossing the river. Gordon was therefore ordered to return to York early the next day, and I rode back that night. The affair at Wrightsville had been almost bloodless; Gordon had one man wounded, and he found one dead militiaman, and captured twenty prisoners."[92]

General Early's fertile mind must have been busy on the ride back toward York. He had followed his orders, destroying the Columbia-Wrightsville Bridge, even though he wanted to save it for his use to capture Lancaster, and then move against Harrisburg. Now he was to return and rejoin General Ewell, who planned a direct assault on Pennsylvania's capital city. It had been a spectacular day for General Early. He had captured the largest city in Pennsylvania that the Confederates would control in the northern invasion. He had done so without firing a shot or losing a man. He came close to capturing the Columbia-Wrightsville Bridge, which he wanted to use to his advantage. The Federal forces that were there to protect it had destroyed it.

General Early had plenty to contemplate on his way back to York that Sunday night. Most likely, his mind was busy as he

---

[92] Jubal A. Early, Lieutenant General Jubal Anderson Early C. S. A. Autobiographical Sketch and Narrative of The War Between The States, with Notes by R. H. Early. J. B. Lippincott Company, Philadelphia & London, 1912. Page 260-261.

rode west. Chewing on a tobacco quid, the General considered everything that happened this day. And probably, his mood was turning more sour. His prize – the captured Columbia-Wrightsville Bridge -- lay at the bottom of the Susquehanna River.

Late that evening, the Confederates camped in the nearby fields of the Detwiler farm. The Kreutz Creek provided water for the tired soldiers and their animals. There was ample firewood for their night's campfires. They were exhausted from the day's marching, skirmishing, and fighting fires.

Only Confederate provost guards remained within Wrightsville overnight, primarily posted to protect the homes whose occupants had fled. Everything remained quiet throughout the night.

In Columbia, a nervous calm remained. The burning of the bridge stopped the Confederates from crossing the Susquehanna that Sunday night. But there were a supply of regular canal boats. The Southerners were indeed only a mile away. Colonel Frick's men encamped at Lockard's Meadow and uneasily tried to catch some sleep. The commanders posted guards along the Susquehanna River. They nervously watched the water. They looked for Confederates scouts that might attempt to cross the river via the canal's dam or on rafts or in boats. In the morning, they knew there could be a full wave amphibious invasion onto the eastern shore of the Susquehanna.

While it was a day full of activity in Wrightsville and Columbia, events to the west and south were rapidly moving forward. It had been a day when the Civil War had finally come to the Susquehanna river towns. Although the burning of the grand bridge that connected the east and west shores of the Susquehanna can be debated as an event that changed the course of the Civil War, what was happening in Maryland and Washington, D.C. easily overshadowed the defense of the bridge.

It was on this day that Fighting Joseph Hooker, the commanding General of the Army of the Potomac, resigned. He had already started moving the Federal army toward the Cumberland Valley in Pennsylvania. Often criticized as having a headquarters that seemed more like a bar and brothel, Hooker's resignation was rapidly accepted. President Lincoln appointed a Pennsylvanian to take his place. General George G. Meade was placed in charge of the Army of the Potomac. From his headquarters in Frederick, Maryland, General Meade sifted through current reports, and studied maps. He issued orders to have his army march toward him, and bring his cavalry forward.

Confederate General Robert E. Lee accepted the word of sometimes actor, sometimes spy James Harrison that the entire Army of the Potomac was moving northwest toward the Cumberland Valley. The Confederate spy Harrison, employed by Lieutenant General James Longstreet, told of the close proximity of the Federals.

General Lee realized that his supply wagons and communications could be cut. General Lee also knew that his invading army was too widely scattered. So he decided to turn his entire army toward a small town that most people in the United States had yet to hear off. Lee started consolidating his entire army at Gettysburg. He decided against attacking Harrisburg, but turned his forces toward the seat of Adams County. There they would regroup, and engage the Army of the Potomac.

It would also soon require General George Meade to concentrate his Federal forces in the area. He was planning where to best position his Army. He hoped to locate ground favorable to his men, fortify that position, and then lure the Confederates to spend itself in attacks against his entrenched forces.

This was the lesson he had learned six months previous at Fredericksburg, and it was still fresh in General Meade's mind. It was a prelude to a coming battle.

The skirmish in Wrightsville lasted about 1½ hours. During that time, the commanders of the bridge defenders did an excellent job in organizing the retreat, especially when considering they were under fire at the time. In comparison, General Gordon failed to follow their withdrawal close enough, thus allowing all but about two dozen men to escape.

Worse, Gordon allowed the bridge to be destroyed. As it smoldered in ruins, so did the General Early's plan to capture Lancaster, and extract a large bounty, before advancing onto Harrisburg.

Although General Gordon succeeded in getting the militia to withdraw from their entrenched positions, they remained intact, and were a force in which he would have had to contend, should he opted to cross the Susquehanna. He also never gained control of the bridge.

From Wrightsville's main street, looking east. The pillars of the bridge destroyed on June 30, 1863 are clearly visible beside the current Rt. 462 bridge.

Looking under the Route 462 bridge arch, the piers from the Columbia-Wrightsville Bridge destroyed on June 30, 1863 are visible and still standing in the Susquehanna. In the distance, the modern Route 30 bridge can be seen in the photograph.

Major Granville O. Haller.

A lone Confederate Soldier's grave is approximately 2 miles north of Wrightsville along Susquehanna River. The unknown is buried within a few feet of River Drive.

Chapter 8
The Days after the Fire

Monday morning was quiet. It was foggy. As daylight cleared away the morning haze, the citizenry on both sides of the river gazed at the Susquehanna. They could see clearly where the bridge was. All that remained were stone pillars. It was a sight of utter ruin.

Downstream, some enterprising Confederates tested crossing the Susquehanna. With the bridge gone, it was a novel idea. They were going to cross the river by walking on the top of the low dam, located down river of where the bridge stood.

The dam was too narrow for Confederate artillery pieces. From their position, the Southerners saw the Federal artillery perched on the eastern bank, awaiting their advance. Without their cannons, it would be impossible. They surmised there might be a place where the river could be forded, but again, they needed their artillery. Wading across the Susquehanna, if possible, would not be easy. Attacking the eastern shore of the Susquehanna without support from their artillery would be next to impossible. As they waded through the river, they gave up and turned around. They were, however, the invading Confederate troops that reached farther east on northern soil than any other throughout the War.

On the eastern shore of the Susquehanna, Colonel Frick and Major Haller rode around Columbia planning how to position their troops, in case the Confederates decided to cross the river in boats or rafts. The made sure their soldiers remained alert, watching the river for river boats filled with Confederates. Fresh brewed coffee stained the morning air. They sipped and watched. So far, there were no sign of the Southerners.

They knew there was ample lumber in Wrightsville – before the bridge fire – that would have easily allowed the Southerners to build such vessels. Over the past several years, the Federals learned how the Confederate army skillfully improvised all kinds of methods of crossing rivers. From building new bridges, ferries, and pontoon crossing, the Confederates proved wily and clever in crossing natural waterways. The only thing that remained between their small defensive force and General Gordon's Confederates was the flowing Susquehanna. Everyone waited for an amphibious assault.

The Chief Burgess of Wrightsville, James F. Magee, sent his daughter, Mrs. Luther L. Rewalt, to locate General Gordon and offered him to stay in his home. The general accepted the offer. General Gordon established his headquarters in Wrightsville at 247 Hellam Street.

General Gordon would later call Mrs. Rewalt "the heroine of the Susquehanna." Mrs. Rewalt's home was one that the Confederates saved from burning.

"I met Mrs. Rewalt the morning after the fire had been checked," General Gordon said[93]. "She had witnessed the furious combat with the flames around her home, and was unwilling that those men should depart without receiving some token of appreciation from her. She was not wealthy, and could not entertain my whole command, but she was blessed with an abundance of those far nobler riches of brain and heart which are the essential glories of exalted womanhood."

General Gordon, known for his striking and handsome good looks, recalled that Mrs. Rewalt was accompanied by an attendant, and at a late hour of the night, sought him, in the confusion, which "followed the destructive fire, to express her gratitude to the soldiers of my command and to inquire how long we would remain in Wrightsville."

Following her father's direction, she found the Confederate General, and spoke with him. She was determined to thank the General for the assistance his men provided in saving Wrightsville from fire. She was the wife of Dr. Luther L. Rewalt, a surgeon in the Union army.

---

[93] John B. Gordon, Reminiscences of The Civil War (New York: Scribner's, 1903), 148-149.

"On learning that the village would be relieved of our presence at an early hour the following morning, she insisted that I should bring with me to breakfast at her house as many as could find places in her dining-room," General Gordon said. "She would take no excuse, not even the nervous condition in which the excitement of the previous hours had left her. At a bountifully supplied table in the early morning sat this modest, cultured woman, surrounded by soldiers in their worn, gray uniforms. The welcome she gave us was so gracious, she was so self-possessed, so calm and kind, that I found myself in an inquiring state of mind as to whether her sympathies were with the Northern or Southern side in the pending war."

General Gordon still wondered about the mysterious note he had been handed the day before in York. Perhaps, he pondered, she was the mysterious author of the note in the bouquet of flowers.

That Monday morning at the breakfast table, the Confederate General's curiosity got the best of him. He pushed Mrs. Rewalt with pointed questions, trying to see if she was the one that penned the note.

It did not take long for the dashing General Gordon to realize that she was not the one that wrote the note. Her responses told him clearly that she was a loyal Union woman.

"Cautiously, but with sufficient clearness to indicate to her my object, I ventured some remarks which she could not well ignore and which she instantly saw were intended to evoke some declaration upon the subject. She was too brave to evade it, too self-poised to be confused by it, and too firmly fixed in her convictions to hesitate as to the answer," General Gordon said. "With no one present except Confederate soldiers who were her guests, she replied, without a quiver in her voice, but with womanly gentleness."

"General Gordon, I fully comprehend you, and it is due to myself that I candidly tell you that I am a Union woman. I cannot afford to be misunderstood, nor to have you misinterpret this simple courtesy," Mrs. Rewalt answered. "You and your soldiers last night saved my home from burning, and I was unwilling that you should go away without receiving some token of my appreciation. I must tell you, however, that, with my assent and approval, my husband is a soldier in the Union army, and my constant prayer to Heaven is that our cause may triumph and the Union be saved."

In Columbia, the lookout vigil continued. Martial law was declared and imposed on the town. It was feared that the Confederate's artillery would shell Columbia, burning it to the ground. Citizens banned together, and started digging rifle pits to defend the borough[94].

The Union troops carefully maintained a lookout on the river, waiting for Confederates to cross the Susquehanna and wade ashore. So far, there was no sign of them. All the canal boats had been taken from the Susquehanna's western shore, and had been moved over to Columbia. Still, as far as the people and soldiers in Columbia knew, there was plenty of lumber available in Wrightsville. They feared the Confederates were building rafts.

General Gordon ordered his men to proceed west toward York. For whatever reason, the Confederates did not destroy the dam that crossed the Susquehanna, or damage the canal at Wrightsville. Either would have disrupted a major freight link between Baltimore and Harrisburg. The Confederates surprisingly allowed both to stand. Gordon led his Georgians west to York, and then on toward Gettysburg, where they would face a greater reckoning with destiny in the coming days.

Before leaving, General Gordon paroled 20 or so Union militia taken as prisoners. At the time, paroled prisoners could no longer fight against the Army that granted the parole.

After the Confederates headed back to York, a group of Wrightsville citizens found a boat, and sailed across the Susquehanna under a white flag. As the boat arrived, many in Columbia feared it was Confederates coming to demand the surrender of the town, or face an artillery shelling. The boat arrived on the Susquehanna's eastern shore in Columbia around 2 p.m., and spread word that the General Gordon and his men had left, marching back toward York. Everyone in Columbia sighed in relief.

---

[94] Columbia Civil War Centennial. A copy is available at the Columbia Historic Society, Columbia, PA. Page 32.

The military commanders maintained their guard of the Susquehanna shoreline.

General Early was back in York demanding his money. He was hell bent on squeezing far more out of the York citizenry. With the Columbia-Wrightsville Bridge burned, he was in a fetid frame of mind. The ever-present scowl on his face was worst than ever. What the citizens there feared most – the burning of their town – was likely once again, now that General Early was no longer paying attention to the capture of the bridge.

He was telling the leaders of York that if he received the balance of the $100,000, his men would not burn the town's factories or the railroad property. What really saved the town was the arrival of a Confederate courier on a galloping horse. He was carrying orders from Confederate General Robert E. Lee to concentrate all forces on the west side of the South Mountain, in Franklin County. General Early read the order, and passed word to his commanders to prepare for a march the next day. General Early did not tell the people of York of his intentions. He preferred to let them remain in turmoil. He was, exactly as General Lee had said, a "bad old boy."

General Early had to be disappointed when he began riding west out of York on Monday. Chewing tobacco, spitting from time to time, he summarized that he had failed to capture the bridge, cross into Lancaster County, or get the sum of money he wanted from the town of York. It was enough to put him into a particularly foul mood. But there was much work ahead of him in Adams County.

A hospital was established at the Columbia Classical Institute[95], located at Fifth and Locusts Streets. Cots were placed in the rooms. The grounds were described "a cool, shady, and a

---

[95] This building was later used as the High School and as a Grammar School.

breezy spot" within the Borough. In service there were "good nurses and skillful physicians." The first floor of the public school room was used a field hospital. A yellow flag floated over the building. It housed the soldiers wounded while holding the Wrightsville entrenchments. Seven or eight were wounded, and some required surgery, but none were mortally wounded. Those soldiers that were sick also were nursed back to health there[96]. The second floor of the Odd Fellows' Hall was also used temporally as a field hospital within Columbia.

On Tuesday, June 30, the Lancaster Intelligencer published, and news of the great bridge fire in Columbia was reported:

Great Excitement!
The Columbia Bridge Burned! – The Enemy at Wrightsville in Force
The Confederates have overrun the entire Cumberland Valley from the Potomac to within three mils of Harrisburg – also the counties Adams and York. On Sunday evening their pickets appeared at Wrightsville, when after a short skirmish, our forces returned across the river and burned the bridge behind them. The Town of York was surrendered by the citizens on Sunday morning. The people of Columbia are flying in all directions, the roads on Sunday night and yesterday being filled with fugitives. There are reports of fighting near Oyster's Point, three miles west of Harrisburg.

The next day, the typesetters of the *Lancaster Express* had more time to set a longer account of what had happened Sunday evening. The newspaper's editor published this account in the July 1 edition:

The Destruction of the Columbia Bridge
The Fight at Wrightsville
Columbia, June 29, 11 A.M.

---

[96] The Columbia Spy, January 16, 1886.

The grand bridge over the Susquehanna which was destroyed last night, was constructed in 1834 and cost $157,000. It was 5,629 feet long, fourteen feet above high water, built of all wood, and about forty feet wide; had two tracks, also, used for vehicles and foot passengers, and tow paths, the latter for the Susquehanna and Tide Water Canal.

The configuration was a sublime sight, the entire length being on fire at once, with the buildings at Wrightsville and floating blasting timbers in the stream. The rebels were on the other bank and the adjacent hills, and crowds of males and females on this side glaring at the sight. The fire department here was in service constantly to save the eastern end of the bridge, but it was useless. Soldiers, citizens, and freeman labored together, also the Philadelphia City Troop. The troop acted splendidly in the fight. The only Columbia volunteers in the fight were fifty-three negroes, who, after making entrenchments with the soldiers, took muskets and fought bravely.

The retreat of the troops, the firing of the bridge, and the shell and shot falling into the river, created a panic here, and the skedaddle continued during the night as the shelling of the town was anticipated.

Colonel Frick and Major Haller had artillery posted at different points on the bank, under Lieutenant Ridgeway, to use a necessary. Major Haldeman, of Columbia, as a volunteer aid, acted nobly. We had no artillery in the entrenchments. Before the fight piles of lumber and empty freight cars were placed in Wrightsville to check the enemy, and were successful. The rebel force was about eight thousand, consisting of infantry, artillery, and a regiment of cavalry. They played upon us with six pieces of artillery. Companies A, G, E, C, and L, of Colonel Thomas' Regiment are missing and believed to be captured. Companies B, F, and H, were in the fight but safe. D, I, K, and M, are with the Colonel at Bainbridge. The quartermaster, with about two hundred men, is in Lancaster; among them Sergeant Evans and seven of Company C. Captain March was wounded in the leg and arm slightly. Lieutenant Colonel Sickles and one Lieutenant are reported captured.

The engagement commenced by skirmishing on the left, on the railroad, between a small squad and fifty rebel dismounted cavalry. Major Knox was there and narrowly escaped being hit. Our squad fell back to the entrenchments fighting. Half an hour afterwards the pickets on the turnpike, a mile from the entrenchments, were attacked and retired, followed by the enemy.

In a few moments three pieces of artillery were planted on the pike, about five hundred yards from the entrenchments, and three in a field to the right. At the same time it was discovered that we were flanked on both sides. Our forces engaged comprised the 27th Regiment, three companies of the 20th, an independent Maryland company, detachments of convalescents, Caption Walker's company of the 26th, and a negro company. The rebel artillery fire was continuous, the shells bursting within the entrenchments. After a gallant defense without artillery, the order fir retreat was given, and in good order, we retired, the enemy's cavalry following to the bridge entrance, and shells bursting all around. The colors formerly of the 129th Pennsylvania waved during the fight, and small flags were waving here and there along the lines. Nothing was lost except a few tents, rations, and entrenching tools.

The order from Harrisburg to prevent the rebels from crossing was imperative, and the destruction of the bridge was absolutely necessary. The first toll-house on the York turnpike was within the centre of the entrenchments. Caption Smith, Company A, 27th Regiment, narrowly escaped a shell, and Company E, covered the retreat magnificently. Serg't Steadman was surrounded, but escaped. The rebel loss is unknown, but several were seen to fall.

At noon on Saturday, Colonel Jenning's regiment was at York Springs, Fourteen miles north of Hanover, retreating towards Harrisburg. The rebels were close on eight abreast with a large wagon train. General Ewell knows the country, having formerly visited here.

On Saturday four companies of Thomas' regiment were attacked by two hundred mounted riflemen at a bridge eight below York but they drove the enemy back. Subsequently, however, they were reported captured.

Since the above was in type three companies have arrived in Lancaster, and will report to Col. Thomas at Bainbridge.

General Early managed to move his Southerners back to Gettysburg in time to participate in the three days of the Battle. Approaching the town from the north, General Early's positioned his division on the rightmost flank of the Confederate line. His men soundly defeated Union General Francis Barlow's division, which was part of the Union XI Corps, in assaults on July 1, 1863.

General Early's men inflicted three times the casualties to the Federal defenders as they suffered. On the first day of the Battle of Gettysburg, his men drove the Union troops back through the streets of town, capturing many of them. During the second day at Gettysburg, he assaulted East Cemetery Hill as part of Ewell's efforts on the Union right flank. Despite initial success, Union reinforcements arrived to repulse Early's two brigades. On the third day, Early detached one brigade to assist Edward "Allegheny" Johnson's division in an unsuccessful assault on Culp's Hill.

General Early remained defiant as ever. When General Lee surrendered, General Early rode a horse to Texas. He hoped to find and join another Confederate force. Disguised as a farmer, General Early fled to Mexico, and from there sailed to Cuba, then onto Canada. Living in Toronto, the wily Confederate wrote *A Memoir of the Last Year of the War for Independence, in the Confederate States of America*. In 1868, General Early received a pardon from President Andrew Jackson. The following year, he returned to Virginia, and resumed his law practice. He became the first president of the Southern Historical Society, and became the most vocal of the Lost Cause movement. General Early publicly blamed General James Longstreet for the loss of the Battle of Gettysburg.

Although most of General Early's soldiers referred to him as "Old Jube" with enthusiasm and affection, his subordinate generals often felt little of this adoring affection. Early was an inherent faultfinder, offering biting criticism of his subordinates at any opportunity. Blind to his own mistakes, he reacted fiercely to criticism or suggestions. The end for General Early came three decades later. On March 2, 1894, he fell down a flight of steps. He was 77 when he died in Lynchburg, Virginia. He was buried in the Spring Hill Cemetery.

By the second week of July, the Federals transported some Rebels captured at Gettysburg through Columbia. They were on their way to Fort Delaware. A small local boy started an enterprise of feeling canteens for the captured Confederates. He reportedly delights in telling the gray suits about the fall of Vicksburg.

"Hey Johnny, do you know Vicksburg is taken?" he cheerfully informed the dirty, smelly men in route to a Federal prison camp south of Philadelphia.

General Couch was ordered, in late July, to issue an order dismissing Major Granville Haller. The Secretary of War signed Special Orders No. 331 on July 25, 1863, ordering one of the heroes that defended Wrightsville and Columbia from the service. Major Haller would spend years trying to reclaim his good name. The dismissal had nothing to do with his actions in defense of his native Pennsylvania, but rather over a questionable toast to the south in front of a naval officer the previous year. Major Haller denied making any such remarks. His actions during the last two weeks of June, 1863, certainly did not make him appear to be a Southern sympathizer by any stretch of the imagination.

It did not take long before there were cases of neighbor turning against neighbor. Within two weeks after the destruction of the Columbia-Wrightsville Bridge, and with no imminent danger from the Confederates, charges and counter charges were aired, some which made it into the local press.

The command at Harrisburg was maligned its failure to provide properly manned artillery to aid in the local defense at Wrightsville and Columbia. A Wrightsville citizen was accused of firing on the retreating Union militia. Citizens of Columbia were accused of being cowards, too quick to flee and refused to assist in the common defense of their borough. The surrender of York was criticized and offered as evidence of strong Southern sympathy.

Editors of local presses had a field day, describing the Confederates' march through the streets of York as a welcome, rather than as regret. York papers countered that the actions of their town's leaders were unavoidable, and necessary, to prevent the destruction of the city.

Mrs. DeWolf of Wrightsville, with others, reportedly fired a revolver at Union soldiers as they headed toward the bridgehead. It was a charge that vehemently denied as a falsehood and slander.

There was a dispute as to whether or not the residents of Wrightsville displayed a white flag of truce. Some reports reflected that flag was waved only after the last Union soldier entered the bridge. Upon seeing it with his field glasses, a Confederate commander ordered the shelling stopped. Others disputed the story.

Someone believed that a Confederate officer seen with General Gordon had been in York two weeks earlier, drinking at a bar. The "spy" was obviously gathering information, or at least, that was the conjecture.

A county correspondent published in the York local press on July 3, 1863, that "The City Troop is condemned for the cowardly manner in which they 'covered' the retreat from Wrightsville, on Sunday night. Instead of 'covering' the rear, the gallant City Troop reached the eastern end of the bridge, fifteen minutes in advance of the infantry, thus covering themselves with shame and disgrace. The Troop are an independent body of tacticians and therefore go it on their own and 'skedaddle' when it best suits their purpose."

The July 7 issue of the *York Gazette*, carried this item:

"The slanders of York, who seem to regret that our beautiful borough was not laid in ashes by General Early (and we regret to say that such wretches still reside in our midst) persist in their misrepresentations. We can only say that we gave what he believed to be a truthful and impartial narration of all the circumstances in our last issue. Statements that the Railroad gave a large amount of money to save their property here, and others of like character are totally false. The people, conscious of their defenseless position, submitted to imperious necessity, and in saving their lies and property, did what humanity and common sense dictated. The whole amount of money and supplies, furnished the Rebels, in compliance with their requisitions amount in the aggregate to some $36,000.00. All good citizens, while they deplore the humiliation of the occupation of our town by the enemy, ad grateful for our escape from the horrors of war."

The allegations of being a copperhead, charges, and counter-charges, appeared in the area newspapers. The allegations made many local citizens suffer humiliation. Time never healed all the wounds caused by the distrust of former friends under the stress of the War.

A memorial erected in Millersville to remember the students of the Normal School who died during the war with connections to the school. Some of the militia that defended the Columbia-Wrightsville Bridge were raised from the school. The monument stands on the grounds of the Millersville University on George Street.

Chapter 9
The Claim for Damages

With the Battle of Gettysburg over and the Confederates driven back to Virginia, it was time for Pennsylvanians to rebuild the damage to their state. The bridge that spanned between Columbia and Wrightsville had economic value. It was privately owned, built with the intention of an investment generating revenue by collecting tolls.

Owned by the Columbia Bank and Bridge Company, they wanted paid for their loss. They looked to the U.S. Army for reimbursement of their loss.

Concern about the economic loss to the bridge was a concern a week before it was burned. In a letter to General Couch, the cashier of the local bank inquired about whether or not the bridge might be destroyed:

COLUMBIA BANK,
Columbia, Lancaster Co., Pa., July 3, 1863.
Major-General D. N. COUCH.
DEAR SIR: The bridge across the Susquehanna at Columbia, Lancaster County, Pennsylvania, is owned by the Columbia Bank, of which I am cashier. I beg leave to enquire, and respectfully request your answer in writing, whether the following order to Major C. C. Haldeman, or any other given by you, authorizes him or any other person to destroy or burn it in any event?

HEADQUARTERS OF THE
DEPARTMENT OF THE SUSQUEHANNA,
June 15, 1863.
Captain C. C. Haldeman, of Columbia, Pa., is hereby authorized to raise troops and assumed command of the same for the

defense of Columbia, Pa., the bridges, dams, and fords on the Susquehanna River in the vicinity.

By order of D. N. COUCH,

Major- General, Commanding.

"John G. Shultze, Acting A. A. G."

Very respectfully,

Samuel Shock, Cashier.

It is unclear whether General Couch ever answered Samuel Shock's letter. Most likely, he did not respond, especially considering the state of emergency. There is no record or mention anywhere that General Couch had been able to respond prior to the actual destruction of the Columbia-Wrightsville Bridge.

There was obvious concern over the financial stability of the Columbia Bank following the bridge's destruction. On June 29, the day following the fire, Samuel Shock[97], wrote a letter to the newspaper editors. He said, "Dear Sir - The bridge at this place, owned by the Columbia Bank, was burned by the United States military authorities, to prevent the rebels from crossing the Susquehanna. The loss will not affect the credit of the Bank." His letter was published July 8 issue of the *Lancaster Examiner & Herald.*

Local newspaper editors began questioning the destruction. A week later, in the July 7 issue of the *Lancaster Intelligencer*, an article ran about fire:

> The Columbia Bridge. – This bridge, which was destroyed by our forces on Sunday night week, was one of the most extensive structures of the kind in this country. The first bridge erected at Columbia was destroyed by a freshet in 1832. It cost upwards of $200,000. The one lately burned was built by the Columbia Bank in 1934, which fully sustained it credit then, as it has done ever since. It costs $159,000, on which there was an insurance of $50,000. The bridge answered a three-fold purpose, at it had a passenger track, a railroad track, and a towing path outside, on which boats navigating The Tide Water Canal were towed across the Susquehanna. The destruction of the bridge would seem to have been rash and un-

---

[97] Also sometimes spelled Schock.

necessary, as tearing up of the plants at the southern end would have been sufficient to prevent any crossing by the enemy. The government is responsible for whatever losses may ensue from the burning of the structure.

The local newspaper editor was already second-guessing the military commanders. But now that the bridge had been destroyed, the bank intended upon collecting for its damages. The president of the Columbia Bank (formerly the Columbia Bank and Bridge Company) wrote to General Couch, presenting a claim for the bank's damages:

COLUMBIA BANK, August 13, 1863.
Major-General D. N. Couch,
Commanding Susquehanna Department
DR. SIR:
I beg leave to make the following statement to you in behalf of the Columbia Bank, of which I am the president, viz:
A bridge across the Susquehanna River, at Columbia, was built and owned by the Columbia Bank. It consisted of two stone abutments, twenty-eight stone piers, with a wooden structure and roof thereon, and was put up between the years 1832 and 1834, at a cost of $157,300. It enabled the traveling public to cross with horses, carriages, wagons, &c., and also railroad cars on the great thoroughfare to York and Baltimore, with passengers and freight, by means of a double-track railway thereon.
When the rebels, under General Lee, invaded Pennsylvania they marched through York, York County, and advanced upon Wrightsville, immediately opposite to Columbia. Colonel Jacob G. Frick, who was in command of the troops for the defense of Columbia, took charge of the bridge on or about the '23d of June, 1863, and held it in charge until after the 28th of that month, when, after his troops in York County were driven by the rebels from their rifle pits & forced across this bridge, it was burned, under his express orders, as a military necessity for the safety of Columbia and eastern Pennsylvania. Since that day the travel across the river has been very much interrupted, and is only done by means of flatboats with great delay, while railway travel is entirely stopped. The piers having been coped with oak plank and

iron are now much exposed to danger, as the coping has been destroyed by the fire and must be seriously injured, if not totally removed, by ice the coming winter unless suitable protection be made for them.

Application is now made to you for such redress of the loss sustained by the bank as the case may require, and you are respectfully requested to interpose at an early day in such manner as will be just to the Columbia Bank.

Very respectfully,
BARTON EVANS,
Prest. Columbia Bank.

President Barton received a prompt and terse reply from General Couch fifteen days later:

H'DQUARTERS, DEP'NT OF SUSQUEHANNA,

Chambersburg, Pa., Aug. 28th, '63.
As stated within, this bridge was burned by my orders as a most positive military necessity.
D.N. Couch, Maj. Gen.

I decline ordering the rebuilding of this bridge.
D.N. Couch, Maj. Gen.

Barton obviously moved forward with plans to rebuild the bridge, and solicited an estimate to rebuild the structure. On September 21, 1863, a master bridge builder, S.W. Mifflin sent a letter and estimate to the bank:

Columbia, Sep. 21, 1863
To the Directors of the Columbia Bank.
GENTLEMEN:
I herewith submit an estimate of the cost of erecting stone piers similar in number & size & quality to those of the bridge recently burnt.

The top of each pier is 10 feet wide by 36 feet long, descending 7 feet to a skew back with a batter of two inches per foot at the sides & one inch at the ends. Each skew back is 6 inches wide.

The icebreaker starts at the skew back and descends at angle of 45 degrees on the upper end. All the other faces of the pier & ice breaker have a hatter of one inch per foot. The average depth of the water before the dam was built was about 3 feet at low water. The dam raised it 6 feet; it is now about two feet above low water, & the top of the pier is 24 feet above the present surface, making 35 feet for the average height of the piers.

From these data it results that the contents of each pier are 1,046 perches, and the total contents of piers & two abutments are 31,380 perches.

To ascertain the cost per perch is rather more difficult, depending as it does so much on the facility of procuring stone.

If stone of good quality could be had on the immediate bank of the river the work could be built for five dollars per perch. I have built as good for four dollars when wages were twenty per cent lower than at present. But the bad character of the stone around Columbia is well known & would add greatly to the expense of procuring so large a quantity.

If you add another dollar for transportation, you are probably safe. At least it would be safe to rate it between $5 & $6 dollars & the whole cost between $156,900 & $188,280.

Respectfully submitted,
S. W. MIFFLIN, C. E.

Mifflin added this estimate to his correspondence:

SAML. W. MIFFLIN,
Civil Enqineer.
To the Directors of the Columbia Bank:
GENTLEMEN: I here present you with an estimate of the cost of rebuilding the Columbia bridge according to the original plan of that structure.

Materials for one span of 200 ft. long:
101,000 feet bill timber, $25 per M $2,525.00
29,000 feet floor plank, $25 per M
725.00

6,000 feet weather-boarding, $25 per M
150
12,000 feet lineal, roofing laths, $5 per M
60
25,000 shingles, $18
450
1,000 lbs. iron bolts, 7c.
    70

1,500 lbs. nails and spikes Sc	75
Total cost material	$4,055
Labour:	
900 days carpenter work, $2.50	$2, 250
350 days, laborers, $1.75	475
200 days, horses, 75	150
	$6,930

Making a cost of $34.65 per lineal foot.

The length of your bridge as given me by your president is 5,860 feet, which, estimated at $35.00 per foot, will amount to ($205,100.00) two hundred and five thousand one hundred dollars.

If it he proposed to adapt the bridge to the passage of locomotives without changing the piers, I would four trusses instead of three, having the timbers differently arranged so as to bring them within a thickness of two feet each. This plan would leave a clear opening in the middle of 10 feet for a railway and two side passages of 9½ feet each for common travel.

The additional cost of this arrangement would be as follows:

23,600 ft. Bch. timber, $25	$590
500 lbs. iron rods, 8c	30
105 days carpenter work	262. 50
25 days, laborers	37.50
10 horses	.75
	920.75

or $4.60 per foot.

Adding this to former estimate gives $39.25 per foot for a bridge adapted to locomotives.

For more than five years after the bridge's destruction, all traffic across the river was by ferry. It would not be until 1869 when a bridge reconnected the towns of Columbia and Wrightsville. A replacement covered bridge was completed on March 1, 1869. It was the third bridge to span the Susquehanna, connecting the two river towns. The stone piers built 37 years earlier in 1832 were reused.

The Columbia Bank, changing its name to the Columbia National Bank in 1864 to comply with new banking laws, had sold the bridge piers to the Pennsylvania Railroad for $57,000. On July 12, 1864, the Columbia Bank transferred its interest in the bridge piers and franchise to the Pennsylvania Railroad Company. The railroad made three payments, the first of $7,000, then two additional payments of $25,000 each. The Columbia National Bank was now out of the bridge business, no longer collecting tolls, but tried to collect for the damage to the bridge it own until June 28, 1863.

In July 1865, committees from the Boroughs of Wrightsville and Columbia had appealed to the Pennsylvania Railroad Company for the immediate rebuilding of the bridge. The railroad blamed the high cost of labor and materials for the delay.

In 1868, the postponed construction finally commenced on the third bridge. It was to be built across that same point in the Susquehanna, erected on the stone piers of the second burned bridge. That third bridge lasted until the early morning hours of Wednesday, September 30, 1896. An unforgiving hurricane slammed Columbia, and sometime around 1 a.m., severe winds and rains ravaged the bridge. It was soon swept from its piers and thrown into the river, a massive splintered ruin. The piers defied destruction.

The Pennsylvania Railroad Company built the fourth bridge to span the Susquehanna between Columbia and Wrightsville. That bridge was constructed of iron and steel. Work was started on April 16, 1897, and amazingly, was completed on May 11. The project was considered to be the fastest bridge-erecting job in the world at that time. One of the 200-foot spans actually was erected in just 8½ working hours. It opened for traffic on June 7, 1897. It remained Columbia's uncompleted bridge, because it was designed for two decks. The top deck was never completed. For years, the bridge served passenger traffic from York to Philadelphia. Each day, Train 5504 and 5505 ran between the two points, and cross the Susquehanna on this bridge.

By the late 1920's, vehicular traffic was jammed, trying to cross the bridge, in between train crossings. The state contracted with the Wiley-Maxon Construction Company to build the fifth bridge in May 1929. On Tuesday, September 30, 1930, the concrete bridge opened to vehicular traffic. It is the world's longest concrete multiple-arch bridge. Known today as Route 462, it was originally Route 30, and part of the great Lincoln Highway. A sixth bridge, a modern concrete structure, was built in the 1970's further north, and today carries Route 30 traffic.

Over the years, the Columbia National Bank continued to press its claim for damages. Congress would eventually introduce bills authorizing the payment for the bridge. The claim was then tabled by a congressional committee, or presented to a Court of Claims. In 1904, the matter was still unsettled. Depositions were taken of those that were still alive. But many of key people – General Couch, Colonel Frick, Captain Haldeman – had died. Lawyers raised questions, each trying to prove a minuet point. Clearly, the bridge was destroyed in the defense of Lancaster County against the Confederate invasion. The military forces defending the bridge had ordered its destruction.

Congress, in its wisdom, tabled the damage claim. There was never any authorization for the loss to the grand covered bridge.

The Columbia Bank was never paid for its loss to its bridge on June 28, 1863. At simple 6% interest, the claim today would be worth well over $170 million in today's dollars. The Columbia National Bank eventually went out of business. Its building, as well as the stone piers in the Susquehanna it once owned, remains present and visible today. The bank building sits mostly dormant, although recently is has been purchased and is being turned into a museum.

The stone piers of the grand bridge are just north of of the fifth, Route 462 bridge. They remain in the river, having been able to withstand the rapid water and winter ice jams, and so far, time itself. Truly, a testament of the detailed knowledge and advanced skills of the early bridge builders, it is easy to forget how many decades the piers have remained in the Susquehanna River.

Those formidable and durable stone piers that exist today remain the most tangible piece of evidence of the earlier bridge. They remind visitors to the river of the once grand bridge that stood there. Their very existence begs the questions of "what if?"

What if Confederate General Early had managed to capture the bridge and crossed it? Would he have punished Lancaster and captured Harrisburg?

What if the bridge defenders had not slowed down General Gordon? Would that have had an effect at the Battle of Gettysburg three days later? Civil war scholars and military experts debate that topic to this day. Had General Early crossed the Susquehanna, captured Lancaster, and turned toward Harrisburg, would General Lee have focused an attack on the Federal forces at Gettysburg? What would have happened if there had not been a Battle of Gettysburg? If the Southerners had captured the Northern capital of Harrisburg, what would have Abraham Lincoln done?

What if the bridge had been replaced quickly? What effect did the delay have on the local economy? Would Columbia and Wrightsville be much larger cities today? Would they have served as an important generator of commerce?

What if Congress had authorized the payment for the damage to the bridge? Could Columbia and Wrightsville have grown into a more vibrant center of commerce? Or did the residents and business miss the opportunity of enterprise during Reconstruction because of the broken transportation link? Why did Congress refuse to pay for the damage? Would the Columbia National Bank still exist today?

All these questions – and probably scores more – could be discussed for days. All because of a covered bridge that existed, and for the most part, has been forgotten to history.

Just like the early peoples known as the Susquehannocks and the Conestoga that once roamed the land, the longest covered bridge in the world is now gone forever. Its defenders -- they too are gone -- and many of their names are lost in history. At this defense, Black American troops were tested – and stood fast – to stop the overwhelming superiority of the Confederate forces. Their deed should never be forgotten.

But they were all there before us, and because of that, became part of our heritage that should never be forgotten. What they did in 1863 changed the course of American history.

The Columbia National Bank Building, as it stands in Columbia today. It has recently been used as a museum.

Appendix

Report of Major Granville O. Haller, Seventh U. S. Infantry.

YORK, PA., July 21, 1863.

GENERAL:

I have the honor to submit the following details in connection with the defense at the Columbia Bridge:

The troops from York, under my charge, arrived at Wrightsville about 7.30 p. m. A scene presented itself which can hardly be exaggerated. Locomotives, tenders, and cars of all descriptions lined the railroad, awaiting removal to Columbia.

The turnpike road leading to the bridge was lined with large wagons, removing property of citizens across the Susquehanna. There was much time lost by teamsters having to halt and pay toll and the transportation agents not having sufficient animals for the extraordinary demands upon them.

Having obtained quarters for my command and arranged for their suppers, I sought Dr. [Barton] Evans, president of the bridge company, and pointed out the detention at the bridge, and, the removal by our people being involuntary, urged that tolls should not be exacted. The president at once threw the bridge open to travel free. I then authorized, in your name, the transportation agents to impress teams to remove the rolling stock, when the crossing became exceedingly active. All night long the work went on, and I am happy to say everything was passed over safely excepting one car, which seemed to have been left designedly, as I repeatedly urged its removal.

I sought for Col. J. G. Frick, commanding Twenty-seventh Pennsylvania Militia, whose regiment was guarding the approaches from York, and at a very late hour met him. I found him confident of the courage of his troops, and eager to resist anything like a raid to destroy the bridge. We then arranged to throw up rifle-pits and use every precaution to save the bridge that our forces would enable us to do. He sent at once for intrenching tools, and early next morning the colonel, Maj. C. C. Haldeman, and myself examined the approaches, and traced out the line of rifle-pits and positions for our troops.

To prevent the enemy crossing the Columbia Bridge, I arranged and relied upon the following defenses:

1. Two Napoleon guns and one iron rifle piece, placed in battery in Columbia, to rake the bridge in case the enemy forced it while our troops were relying on other defenses. These guns were manned by a detachment of the Twenty-seventh Pennsylvania Militia, under Lieutenant [Delaplaine J. Ridgway, and some citizens of Columbia. There was also a small guard of the Twenty-seventh Pennsylvania Militia at the Columbia side of the bridge.

2. The fourth span (from Wrightsville) of the bridge was selected, and mechanics were employed to separate the roof and sides, leaving only "the arches and a very small portion of the lower chords" for crossing over. lit was expected that holes bored into these arches and filled with powder would, by exploding the powder, shiver the timber and cause the span, about 200 feet long, to drop into the river, and thus render the bridge useless to the enemy. This work was superintended by Mr. Robert Crane, who had previously, upon the first alarm, begun this work, and who has cheerfully rendered me every assistance. His report * is herewith inclosed, marked A. Lieutenant Randall, of the City Troop, first, and subsequently Maj. C. McLean Knox, Ninth New York Cavalry, was placed by the mines to observe whether the enemy approached, with instructions to order the mines to be exploded in time to prevent them from getting over the doomed arch. I relied very much upon the success of this arrangement.

3. A tete-de-pont immediately around the bridge to cover the re-treat of our troops. A few hopper cars (iron), loaded with iron ore, were retained to barricade the main street leading from York to the bridge. The side streets were obstructed by boards piled together so as to make complete breastworks for defense. This work was performed by the citizens under the directions of Mr. [Samuel H.]Mann, of Wrightsville, the provost-marshal, to whom I indicated the lines of defense. This bridge-head was garrisoned by about 50 of the Twenty-sixth Pennsylvania Militia, very much worn down by their retreat from Gettysburg, and a

small guard at the bridge, of the Twenty-seventh Pennsylvania Militia.

4. About three-fourths of a mile in front of the bridge is a ridge which curves in toward the Susquehanna River, and on the upperside, near the river, beyond this, is another height, both of which are good positions for defense against infantry and cavalry. Two small creeks run at the foot of these eminences. But outside of these, above and below Wrightsville, are ridges making in at right angles to the river which, with artillery, would command these defenses. With the force at our command, it was impossible for us to place troops on these ridges. To defend the bridge successfully, these ridges would have to be occupied by our troops, supported by artillery. It would have required, perhaps, five times our number to have garrisoned the line extending from the upper to the lower ridge.

Our defense, therefore, contemplated resistance to a raid by the enemy's cavalry and mounted infantry which might be thrown for-ward to destroy the bridge. York was not occupied by the enemy until 10 a. m. Sunday, June 28, and it was not known what the enemy's designs were. If they came with a column to invade the county it would be impossible to defend the bridge successfully. We therefore strengthened our position by rifle-pits as far as our supply of tools would permit, determined to hold our ground until the development of the enemy showed a superiority in numbers, aided by cannon.

The extent of Wrightsville and the nature of the ground required a line of defense over 1 mile in length.

To garrison this line we had Col. J. G. Frick's Twenty-seventh Pennsylvania Militia (excluding artillery and bridge guards), 650; York Battalion (invalids and Patapsco Guards), 238; Lieut. Col. William H. Sickles, 3 Companies Twentieth Pennsylvania Militia, 200; total, 1,088. These troops were disposed of as follows:

The Twenty-seventh Pennsylvania Militia, Colonel Frick Commanding, occupied the rifle-pits in front and on both sides the York turnpike, with one company thrown forward on the pike to picket the road.

The York Battalion (Composed of old soldiers, wounded, and convalescents, who have been under fire) was placed under command of Lieutenant-Colonel Green, Twenty-seventh Pennsylvania Militia, and posted on the left of Colonel Frick's regiment, extending to the Susquehanna River, the Patapsco Guards in reserve. This line was most likely to be seriously assailed, as the ground here most favored the enemy's approach.

The battalion of Twentieth Pennsylvania Militia, Lieutenant-Colonel Sickles commanding, guarded the approaches on the right of the Twenty-seventh Pennsylvania Militia to the river.

The Adams County Cavalry were thrown forward on the York pike and neighboring heights to as certain if the enemy approached, and their probable force. About a dozen were sent forward to ob-serve the Old Baltimore road. The City Troop patrolled Wrightsville, and obliged every soldier to repair to his company. A few of the City Troop were selected as messengers, and stationed with the field officers to carry communications.

My information represented York as having been occupied at 10a. m. by 1,000 rebels, and our scouts were driven within our lines without having ascertained the enemy's number or that they had artillery. There was reason to hope that their number was not formidable, and we might save the bridge. However, as the enemy approached, they presented a deployed line of cavalry and infantry skirmishers, which spread to the summit of the ridge on our left, and in the distance a mass of infantry was observed.

The enemy advanced very slowly, feeling their way, and occasion-ally firing, which our men returned. The luxuriant grain in the fields in our front and the woods on our left covered the assailants, while our rifle-pits protected our men; hence the firing did but little injury.

For casualties I have to request that battalion commanders be called upon for reports.

As the firing began, I received a telegram * from Col. William B. Thomas, Twentieth Pennsylvania Militia, at Bainbridge, Pa., which is herewith inclosed (marked B), saying: "A scout just arrived from York reports the enemy advancing on Columbia with three brigades of infantry and one regiment of cavalry. If yon," &c. This I deemed it my duty to show to Colonel Frick. The colonel advised retreat, but, dreading confusion when retreating with inexperienced militia, I proposed to the colonel to destroy the span of the Columbia Bridge, thus cutting off all hope of retreat by that route, and hold our ground as long as practicable. We had previously arranged that if cut off from the bridge our retreat should be along the hills bordering the Susquehanna River to some ford above Wrightsville. The Colonel, however, was decidedly of the opinion that we could retreat yet without being hard pressed by the enemy. I accordingly sent an order to Lieutenant-Colonel Sickles to withdraw in good order, and then to Lieutenant-Colonel Green, while Colonel Frick was to fall back as soon as he saw our flanks were well drawn in.

I saw the movement commenced in good order; then hastened to the bridge and saw the mines were ready, and found the artillery in position prepared for the worst.

The enemy had selected positions for their cannon, and, as the re-treat began, opened upon the men and town, firing some 40 rounds. Our retreat was so unexpected to them, so quietly and simultaneously performed, as to disconcert them.

Our troops defiled from the bridge in good order; the companies were promptly formed in the street and the battalion there reformed. An agreeable sight presented itself as the colors of the Twenty-seventh Pennsylvania Militia, held by a sergeant, followed by the regiment in good order, cheering it, marched last from the bridge.

Having selected camping grounds, through the assistance of Maj. C. C. Haldemen the troops were conducted into camp; details were made to guard the river bank; our cannon were provided with horses by impressment, upon your authority (see orders * hereto annexed, marked C), as it was necessary that they should be in readiness to move at a moment's notice. Every precaution was taken to prevent the enemy from crossing to the Lancaster County side.

Our troops reached the bridge in advance of the enemy, and all four men were passed over until the enemy was seen descending the hill, when the mines were exploded. Colonel Frick, who conducted the retreat at the rear, halted at the bridge span to see that the work would be effectually performed.

The explosion unfortunately failed to drop the span into the river, and the enemy's approach required speedy action. Colonel Frick accordingly ordered the bridge to be set on fire, and the seasoned timbers readily took fire, carrying the flames rapidly toward Wrightsville and Columbia.

In Columbia the citizens and soldiers, attracted by the imposing fire, procured axes and entered the bridge to cut away a part of a span. They hoped it would lessen the flames, and by means of the town's fire engines, extinguish the flames before they reached the town, where it would endanger houses and commercial building. The rapidity of the flames and intense heat defeated all their efforts, and the bridge was entirely consumed. Also, a building near it was lost.

The firemen prevented, by their exertions, the spreading of the flames in the town.

In Wrightsville the flames extended to private houses, and the Confederate troops made great exertions to extinguish the fires.

On Monday, June 29, at the request of Colonel Frick, I accompanied him around Columbia on a reconnaissance, and determined the best positions for troops and defenses. This work had just been completed when we received the gratifying intelligence that the enemy had retired from Wrightsville. Soon after I received your telegram directing me to go to Bainbridge at once to see that Colonel Thomas put himself in a position to defend the different fords at every sacrifice, dig pits, make abatis[98], &c. At 2 p. m. I rode up to Chestnut Riffles, and thence to Bainbridge.

Before concluding, I deem it proper to add that Colonel Frick's conduct throughout was zealous and patriotic, and deserves your highest commendation. Lieutenant-Colonel Green, commanding the York Battalion, Captain [Robert] Bell, of the Adams County Cavalry, and Lieutenant Randall, of the City Troop, faithfully obeyed their orders. Maj. Charles McLean Knox, Ninth New York Cavalry, and Mr. Samuel Young, of Reading, gave me every assistance.

I regret to have to add that the conduct of Colonel Sickles and two companies of the Twentieth Pennsylvania Militia deserves investigation. It has been represented to me that the lieutenant-colonel and some 15 or 20 of his men have unnecessarily, but deliberately surrendered to the Confederate troops. Some of the men

---

[98] A defensive obstacle formed by felled trees with sharpened branches facing the enemy.

threw away their arms, and the two companies, without authority, hurried away from Columbia, straggling along the road to Lancaster and filling the country with alarming reports.

The Adams County Cavalry, who were scouting the Old Baltimore road, it seems came into Wrightsville while in the hands of the enemy, and tried to cross the bridge, but found it on fire. They then retreated under the fire of the enemy, having 1 horse shot and a soldier wounded by the fall, but he escaped capture by concealing himself in a house. One soldier and horse were captured. The others reached Safe Harbor in safety, and afterward joined their company.

I have the honor to be, general, very respectfully, your obedient servant,

G.O. HALLER,
Major Seventh Infantry, (late) Aide-de-Camp pro tern.
Maj. Gen. D. N. Couch, Comdg.
Dept. of the Susquehanna, Chambersburg, Pa.

* Not found.

Report of Col. Jacob G. Frick, Twenty-seventh Pennsylvania Militia, of operations June 24—30.

HEADQUARTERS DEFENSES OF LANCASTER COUNTY, Columbia, Pa., July 1, 1863.

CAPTAIN:

I have the honor to report that, in compliance with General Orders, No. 14, from the Department of the Susquehanna, I left Harrisburg on the morning of the 24th ultimo, and arrived here on the afternoon of the same day, and immediately sent four companies, in command of Lieutenant-Colonel Green, over the river.

On the morning of the 25th ultimo, I sent four more companies to that officer, with instructions to take up a position near the York turnpike, about a half mile from Wrightsville.

Hearing, on the afternoon of the 27th, that the enemy were in the vicinity of York, I ordered my two remaining companies to report to Lieutenant-Colonel Green, that we might be prepared to resist any sudden attempt by the enemy to get possession of the bridge at this point.

Late in the evening of the same day, I crossed the river, assumed command, and disposed my force for defense.

During the night, our force was increased by four companies from Columbia (three white and one colored), numbering about 175 men.

Very early next morning, having obtained intrenching tools from citizens of Columbia and the Pennsylvania Railroad Company, my own men and the negro company (the other three companies from Columbia having left for their homes) dug rifle-pits on either side of the turnpike.

During the morning, a detachment of convalescent soldiers from York, and the Patapsco Guards, in all about 250 men, joined me, and they were posted on the left of the town, protecting the left flank of my position. They were placed under command of Lieutenant-Colonel Green. We were also joined by scattered fragments of the Twentieth Regiment Pennsylvania Volunteer Militia, under Lieutenant-Colonel Sickles, during the morning, which I posted on the right of the town as a protection to the right flank.

The work of entrenching was continued until the approach and attack of the enemy, about 5.30 p. in., and, while the work was in progress, I selected, with the assistance of Major Haller, aide-de-camp to the commanding general, the several points at which to post my limited number of men.

The main body of the enemy, about 2,500 strong, composed of cavalry, artillery, and infantry, took up their position about 6 p. m. on the turnpike in our immediate front, and within three-quarters of a mile of our rifle-pits. A force of cavalry and infantry moved down the railroad on our left and attacked our skirmishers, who, after replying to their fire for a short time, retired to the main body, which kept up a steady fire, and held the enemy in check until they received orders to retire to the bridge. The rebels succeeded in getting a battery in position on the elevated ground on our right and a section in our immediate front. These guns were used most vigorously against those of my command occupying the rifle-pits.

In the meantime, they sent a column of infantry, under cover of a high hill on our right, within a few hundred yards of the river. None but their skirmishers approached within range of the guns of the men occupying the rifle-pits, and these being in a grain-field, and obscured from our view, excepting when they would rise to fire, it was difficult to do them much harm or dislodge them. They depended exclusively upon their artillery to drive us from our position here. Having no artillery ourselves on that side of the river with which to reply, and after retaining our position for about one and a quarter hours, and discovering that our remaining longer would enable the enemy to reach the river on both of my flanks, which I was unable to prevent because of the small number of men under my command, and thus get possession of the bridge, cut off our retreat, and secure a crossing of the Susquehanna, which I was instructed to prevent, I retired in good order, and crossed the bridge to the Lancaster side.

Before the enemy had left York for the river here, I made, as I supposed, every necessary arrangement to blow up one span of the Columbia Bridge. When they got within sight, the gentlemen charged with the execution of that work repaired promptly to the bridge, and commenced sawing off the arches and heavy timbers preparatory to blowing it up with powder, which they had arranged for that purpose. After an abundance of time was allowed, and after I supposed every man of my command was over the river, and when the enemy had entered the town with his artillery, and reached the barricade at the bridge-head, I gave the order to light the fuse. The explosion took place, but our object in blowing up the bridge failed. It was then that I felt it to be my duty, in order to prevent the enemy from crossing the river and marching on to Harrisburg in the rear, destroying on his route railroads and bridges, to order the bridge to be set on fire. The bridge was completely destroyed, though a vigorous attempt was made to save a part by the soldiers

I was materially assisted in my operations by Captain Strickler, who had charge of a small force of cavalry, acting as scouts. I feel indebted to him for much reliable information as to the movements and force of the enemy.

Major [Charles C.] Haldeman, formerly of the Twenty-third Regiment Pennsylvania Volunteers, volunteered his services, and rendered me very efficient aid.

Lieutenant-Colonel [David B.] Green, who had charge of the left flank of the position, with a force of 250 men, and Major [George L.]Fried, who took charge of the left wing of the Twenty-seventh Regiment Pennsylvania Volunteer Militia, behaved with accustomed coolness and gallantry, and brought off their forces in most excellent order.

Great praise is due to Captain [Joseph] Oliver, Company D, Twenty-seventh Pennsylvania Volunteer Militia, commanding a body of skirmishers of about 70 men, for the skillfulness and boldness with which he handled his men.

The officers and men of my command generally did their whole duty.

Before closing this report, justice compels me to make mention of the excellent conduct of the company of negroes from Columbia. After working industriously in the rifle-pits all day, when the fight commenced they took their guns and stood up to their work bravely. They fell back only when ordered to do so.

I herewith inclose a list of casualties. *

The prisoners taken—18 in number—were all from the Twentieth Pennsylvania Volunteer Militia, including Lieutenant-Colonel[William H.] Sickles, of that regiment. From information received since the engagement, I feel convinced that if my orders had been promptly obeyed, no prisoners would have been taken.

I have the honor to be, very respectfully, your obedient servant,

JACOB G. FRICK,

Colonel, Commanding.

Capt. ROBERT LE Roy, Asst. Adjt. Gen., Department of the Susquehanna.

General Early's Report

No. 470.

Report of Maj. Gen. Jubal A. Early, C. S. Army, commanding division.

HEADQUARTERS EARLY'S DIVISION,
August 22, 1863.

MAJOR: I have the honor to submit the following report of the operations of this division during the recent campaign, commencing with its departure from Fredericksburg, and ending with its arrival in the vicinity of Orange Court-House:

…A short time before night, I rode out in the direction of Columbia Bridge, to ascertain the result of Gordon's expedition, and had not proceeded far before I saw an immense smoke rising in the direction of the Susquehanna, which I subsequently discovered to proceed from the burning of the bridge in question. On arriving at Wrightsville, on the banks of the Susquehanna, opposite Columbia, I ascertained from General Gordon that, on approaching Wrightsville, in front of the bridge he found a command of militia some 1,200 strong, intrenched, and, after endeavoring to move around their flank to cut them off from the bridge (which he was unable to do from want of knowledge of the locality), he opened his artillery on the militia, which fled at the bursting of the third shell, and he immediately pursued; but as his men had marched a little over 20 miles, on a very warm day, the enemy beat him running. He, however, attempted to cross the bridge, and the head of his column got half way over, but he found the bridge, which had been prepared for the purpose, on fire in the middle. As he had nothing but muskets and rifles, he sent back for buckets to endeavor to arrest the flames, but, before they arrived, the fire had progressed so far that it was impossible to arrest it. He had, therefore, to return, and leave the bridge to its fate.

This bridge was one mile and a quarter in length, the superstructure being of wood, on stone pillars, and it included in one structure a railroad bridge, a pass-way for wagons, and also a tow-path for the canal, which here crosses the Susquehanna. The bridge was entirely consumed, and from it the town of Wrightsville caught fire and several buildings were consumed, but the further progress of the flames was arrested by the exertions of Gordon's men. I regretted very much the failure to secure this bridge, as, finding the defenseless condition of the country generally, and the little obstacle likely to be afforded by the militia to our progress, I had determined, if I could get possession of the Columbia Bridge, to cross my division over the Susquehanna, and cut the Pennsylvania Central Railroad, march upon Lancaster, lay that town under contribution, and then attack Harrisburg in the rear while it should be attacked in front by the rest of the corps, relying, in the worst contingency that might happen, upon being able to mount my division from the immense number of horses that had been run across the river, and then move to the west, destroying the railroads and canals, and returning back again to a place of safety. This project, however, was entirely thwarted by the destruction of the bridge, as the river was otherwise impassable, being very wide and deep at this point. I therefore ordered General Gordon to move his command back to York next day, and returned to that place myself that night.

...Very respectfully, your obedient servant,

J. A. EARLY, Major-General, Commanding Division.

Excerpted from Pages 466-467 – The war of the rebellion: a compilation of the official records of the Union and Confederate armies. / Series 1 - Volume 27 (Part II

Summary of Columbia & Wrightsville's Six Bridges

First Columbia Bridge (Columbia Bridge Company)

Construction started early 1812 and was completed and opened December 5, 1814 at a total cost of $231,771. The bridge was destroyed February 5, 1832 by ice. The builders were J. Wolcott, H. Slaymaker, and S. Slaymaker. It was a covered bridge, built of stone and wood, had 54 piers, and had twin carriageways. The toll was $1.50 for a wagon and 6 horses. Pedestrians were charged 6¢ to cross.

Second Columbia Bridge (Columbia Bank)

Construction mid 1832 and was completed and opened July 8, 1834 at a total cost of $157,300. The bridge was destroyed June 28, 1863 by fire to prevent the Confederate army's advance into Lancaster County. The builder(s) of the bridge were James Moore and John Evans. It was a covered bridge, built of stone and wood, had 27 piers, and included a carriageway, railway, walkway, a towpaths. The toll was $1.00 for a wagon and 6 horses. Pedestrians were charged 6¢ to cross.

Third Columbia Bridge (Pennsylvania Railroad Company)

Construction started in 1868 and the third bridge was opened later that year. It cost the Pennsylvania Railroad Company $400,000 to build the bridge. It was destroyed September 30, 1896 by a hurricane. Built of stone, wood and steel, it had 27 piers, the same as the Second Bridge. A covered bridge, it included a carriageway, railway, and walkway.

Fourth Bridge, Pennsylvania Railroad "Iron" Bridge

Construction started April 16, 1897, and the bridge was opened June 7, 1897. It was used until March 13, 1958. It was finally dismantled for scrap in November 1964. Built of stone and prefabricated steel, it used the same 27 piers as the previous two bridges. It included railway and twin carriageways, which was shared w/ pedestrians. Tolls collected were 20¢ for an automobile, passengers were 4¢, and pedestrians were charged 3¢.

Fifth Bridge, Veteran's Memorial Bridge (Inter-County Bridge)

Construction started in mid 1929, and the bridge was opened September 30, 1930. It is still standing today, and is known as Route 462. It was built by Glen Wiley and Glenway Maxon at a cost of $2,484,000 plus $56,400, which was paid as an early completion bonus. Built of reinforced concrete, it includes 27 river and 22 approach piers. It has a 38' roadway and 6' sidewalk. Tolls were collected when it opened. Automobile were charged 25¢, but the toll was stopped January 31, 1943.

Sixth Bridge, Wright's Ferry Bridge

Constructed started March 1969, and the bridge was opened November 21, 1972. It is still standing today, and is known as Route 30. G.A. & F.C. Wagman, Inc. built the bridge at a cost of $12,000,000. It is built of reinforced concrete and steel, and has 45 piers. It has a divided two-lane roadway. Tolls have never been collected to cross the bridge.

For more information about George Sheldon, visit his website at:

http://www.georgesheldon.com

For more information about Quaker Hills Books, visit their website at:

http://www.quakerhillspress.com

Bibliography

Alleman, (Pierce) Tillie, *At Gettysburg, or What a Girl Saw and Heard of the Battle* (1888) A copy is in the library at Adams County Historical Society, Gettysburg, PA.

Bates, Samuel P., *Martial Deeds of Pennsylvania* (Philadelphia: T. H. Davis & Co., 1876), 168

Broadhead, Sarah *A Diary of a Lady of Gettysburg* Privately printed. A copy is located at the Adams County Historical Society, Gettysburg, PA.

Columbia Civil War Centennial. A copy is available at the Columbia Historic Society, Columbia, PA. Page 13.

Columbia Spy

Diary of William Heyser is located in the University of Virginia Library

Early, Jubal A. *Lieutenant General Jubal Anderson Early C. S. A. Autobiographical Sketch and Narrative of The War Between The States, with Notes by R. H. Early.* J. B. Lippincott Company, Philadelphia & London, 1912

Egle, William H., M.D. *An Illustrated History of the Commonwealth of Pennsylvania, Civil, Political, and Military, From Its Earliest Settlement to the Present Time.* Harrisburg, PA: De Witt C. Goodrich & Co., 1876).

Ellis, Franklin and Evans , Samuel. *History of Lancaster County, Pennsylvania with Biographical Sketches of Many of Its Pioneers and Prominent Men.* Philadelphia: Everts & Peck, 1883.

Fahnestock, Gates D. From a speech given before the National Arts Club of New York, February 12, 1934. A copy is on file at the Adams County Historical Society, Gettysburg, PA

Gordon, John B., *Reminiscences of The Civil War* (New York: Scribner's, 1903),

King, Sarah *A Mother's Story* Published in *The Compiler*, July 4, 1906.

Klein, H.M. J., Ph. D., Editor in Chief. *Lancaster County Pennsylvania, A History.* New York: Lewis Historical Publishing Company Inc. 1924.

Lancaster Examiner & Herald, July 1863 issues.

McClure, James *East of Gettysburg* York: York Daily Record, 2003.

McClure, James *East of Gettysburg* York: York Historic Society, 2003.

McCurdy, Charles M. *Gettysburg: A Memoir.* Reed and Wittin Co., Pittsburgh, PA 1929 P.13. A copy is on file at the Adams County Historical Society, Gettysburg, PA.

Nye, Wilbur S. *Here Come the Rebels!* Louisiana State University Press, Baton Rouge, LA, 1963. 293-284.

Schaefer, Thomas K. *A Matter Never to be Forgotten* York Sunday News, York, PA. 5 June – 17 July, 1988

Stranhan, Susan Q. *Susquehanna River of Dreams.* Baltimore, The John Hopkins Press, 1993.

Sworn depositions of various residents of Columbia and Wrightsville, which were taken in 1904, and part of the record of the Court of Claims, 10492. These records are available at the National Archive. Copies were also provided to the Columbia Historic Preservation Society, Columbia, PA, to be part of their files.

Tagg, Larry, The *Generals of Gettysburg: The Leaders of America's Greatest Battle* El Dorado Hills, CA: Savas Publishing, 1998.

The Press. Philadelphia, PA. Friday, June 26, 1863, issue. Vol. 6 – No. 279. A copy of this article is preserved on microfilm and available at the Pennsylvania State Library, Harrisburg, PA

United States War Department. *The War of the Rebellion: a Compilation of the Official Records of the Union and Confederate Armies, 1880-1891*

Valley Spirit, November 5, 1862.

Will, John C. *Reminiscences of the Three Day Battle of Gettysburg at the Globe Hotel.* An unpublished manuscript on file at the Adams County Historical Society, Gettysburg, PA.

Wrightsville 1736-1976 – Gateway to the West. Published by the Wrightsville Bicentennial Committee in 1976. A copy is on file at the Columbia Public Library.